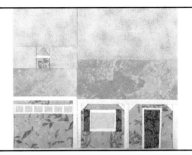

HOMETOWN

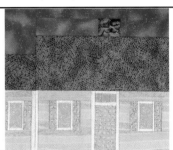

QUILTS

PAPER PIECE A VILLAGE OF MEMORIES

Jodie Davis

Published by

Krause Publications
700 E. State Street
Iola, WI 54990-0001
715-445-2214
www.krause.com

Please call or write for our free catalog of publications. Our toll-free number to place an order or obtain a free catalog is 800-258-0929 or please use our regular business telephone 715-445-2214 for editorial comment and further information.

Library of Congress Catalog Number: 99-66999
ISBN: 0-87341-797-6

Printed in the United States of America

This book is dedicated to the quilters of south Florida who have given me tremendous support through the process of writing the book. And a special thanks goes to the Coral Springs Quilters Guild who welcomed me into their guild so warmly. The quilting world can best be characterized by quilts themselves—warm, inviting, and comforting—and I am truly lucky to make my profession in such a world.

Thanks to the following contributors to the book: Hoffman Fabrics, for the scrumptious batiks used in the Log Cabins quilt, HTC for providing me with Fun-dation, Glenda Irvine for making the Ocean Waves and Barn Yard quilt tops. And, moreover, for her friendship.

Susanne McCoy, Nancy Phelps Goins, Grace Grimsley, June Dale, Marcia Kessler, Margo Antonoff, and Annie Weinstein for their delightful quilts.

And thanks to quilt shops I visited in person and online all over the country for the fabrics I used to create the blocks and quilts.

Table of Contents

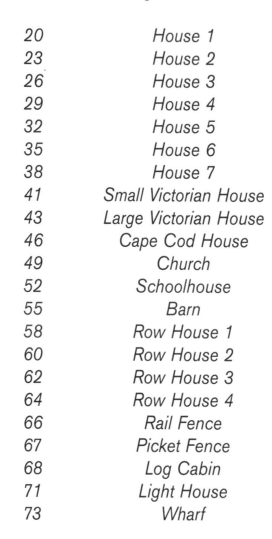

Hometown Quilts & Instructions

Introduction

*n*ow you can create your own village quilt with *Hometown Quilts: Paper Piece a Village of Memories*. It's easy, thanks to foundation piecing.

In this book, you will find 28 blocks designed for you to make your hometown quilt. In addition, I've included appliqué designs to add fun bits of whimsy or pretty highlights of three-dimensional texture to your quilt. My stitch, slash, turn and tack method of appliqué is super easy and quick and creates a great deal of visual interest.

Using the blocks and the appliqués, I've created nine quilts for you with complete instructions. All use one or more of the block designs, some use 3-D appliqués, and some use other fun goodies, such as buttons on the Autumn Quilt. Come up with your own ideas from the toy store or dollhouse shop to add your own style to your quilt.

I hope you'll enjoy the addition of a gallery of quilts made by some of my quilting friends. I was having so much fun creating the blocks I just had to share them. So, two months before my deadline, I made copies of the patterns and made the rounds of a few bees. Gosh, what a warm reception! And then, at the very next guild meeting, there were three finished quilts! I'm sure you will enjoy the different flavors these quilts have. I hoped this would happen—that you'd get more ideas for interpreting my designs thanks to the vision of these talented quilters. Bravo!

Whether you are a veteran quilter or a first timer, do yourself a favor and take some time to give paper piecing a fair trial. Admittedly, it takes a bit of mental gymnastics to "get it" because the technique goes so against the grain of everything we've done as sewers. There are no seam allowances, we're stitching from the back of our work, and the block turns out backwards as a mirror image of the pattern we start out with. Oh boy, this sure could be confusing. But once you "get it" enough to finish the first block, you will discover that paper piecing enables you to piece designs that only the most courageous sewer would tackle using traditional methods. Believe me, I'd never subject myself to piecing these blocks the conventional way—with things like the little windows and window trim. No way!

Grab your scrap basket and let's get going!

Jodie Davis

iejodie@att.net
http//www.iejodie.com

Paper Piecing Primer

THE BLOCK PATTERNS

The patterns in this book are full-size, ready to be photocopied or traced. The numbers on the blocks indicate the sewing sequence for the fabric pieces.

The seam allowance has been added. The outside dashed line is the cutting line and the solid line is the sewing line used for sewing the completed block pieces together.

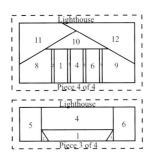

Cutting lines are dashed, sewing lines are solid

Symmetrical Versus Asymmetrical Blocks

You will be sewing from the wrong side of the blocks. The marked side of the foundation is the wrong side. For this reason the finished block will be a mirror image of the block patterns in the book. Notice that for asymmetrical blocks, the photos of the finished blocks are in fact mirror images of the drawn block, whereas for symmetrical blocks there will be no difference between the drawn and sewn blocks. Think backwards.

Symmetrical block   *Asymmetrical block*

FOUNDATION MATERIAL OPTIONS

Foundations can be either permanent or temporary, depending upon the desired end result or working method (hand versus machine).

Permanent Foundations

Permanent foundations remain in the completed quilt, adding an extra layer. The fabrics are stitched to the foundation. Most commonly simple muslin, foundations can also be interfacing or even used dryer sheets. A benefit for some projects (for instance, to add body to a wall hanging or vest), a fabric foundation isn't the best choice for others, such as a project calling for hand quilting or a miniature that shouldn't be too stiff.

If you are purchasing fabric for your foundations, choose a good-quality muslin for your foundation and be sure to cut it square with the grain of the fabric.

Lately I discovered an interfacing-type product made specifically for foun-dation piecing. Fun-dation is packaged either in rolls or in handy pack-ages of 8½" x 11" sheets. It went through my printer beautifully and sews like fabric. I imagine needles don't dull as fast as with paper. Though the manufacturer claims it is tearable, I found it didn't tear crisply, and really, there is no reason to take it out unless one is hand quilting. Besides, why take the extra time? Many of the designs in this book involve many tiny pieces. A permanent foundation eliminates the time-consuming job of tearing paper out of all those small places. To top it off, the price makes it economical as well.

Temporary Foundations

Unlike permanent foundations, temporary foundations are used for piecing the block, but are removed before completing the quilt. They provide the sewing lines and stability for sewing and piecing the blocks together. Many types of paper are used as foundations. Newsprint is the most economical. The characteristics of other materials, such as tracing paper and the slightly more expensive vellum, offer a few important characteristics that make the slight additional expense worthwhile. Both are semi-transparent, thereby allowing you to see the fabrics through the paper—a huge benefit when placing your fabric pieces. And both tear much more easily than regular paper or newsprint. You will appreciate this benefit when the time comes to remove the paper from your blocks.

Transferring the Block Designs

To reproduce the block designs on paper, trace or photocopy them from the book. When tracing, use a ruler to ensure accuracy. Be sure to copy the piecing sequence numbers as well.

A copy machine makes quick work of reproducing block designs. To test the precision of the copies, make one copy of the block and measure to be sure the size matches that of the original. Cut outside the dashed lines.

To transfer block designs to fabric, you may place the muslin over the block design on a light table or tape the design to a sunny window. Trace using a permanent fabric pen. As an alternative, use a heat transfer pen or pencil.

Color-code or mark your patterns so you'll stitch the correct fabric in the proper places in your block. The voice of experience here: When making multiple blocks I make an extra copy of the finished block and color code it as a key so I can easily see where the different fabrics go. You can also mark your actual paper block pieces, though be careful what you mark with.

Blocks In Any Size

It is easy to enlarge the blocks to create blocks of any size you desire. Simply use a copy machine with an enlarging capability. Remember to adjust the seam allowances to 1/4" all around.

Precutting Fabrics

To make piecing less cumbersome, I precut my fabrics into strips or pieces. To judge the size to cut, I place the fabric wrong side down on the block design (since this is how it will be in the finished block) and cut strips about 1" wider than the piece.

If a triangular shape is required, I often precut it as a triangle. This is especially helpful when working with a directional fabric. Make sure you allow even more than the normal 1/2" all around. I'd rather end up cutting away extra fabric instead of ripping out a piece that doesn't fit.

When using new yardage I cut my fabric into strips before I bring them to my sewing table, allowing an extra 1/2" on all edges for a seam allowance and maneuvering room. Yes, there is more waste here than with traditional template cutting, but this method is much faster and allows me to tackle intricate designs, so I don't mind buying a tad bit more fabric. I call this keeping the fabric shops in business!

If you will need half-triangle pieces, cut them from squares or rectangles first. Cut the square or rectangle about 1¼" larger than the finished triangle. Then cut across the diagonal.

Grain Line

One of the beauties of foundation piecing is that the foundation stabilizes the fabrics, thereby mitigating the necessity of following grain line rules strictly. In normal template or rotary cut piecing, it is imperative that the outside edges of blocks be on the straight of grain, or bias stretching will cause problems when piecing blocks together. With foundation piecing, the foundation stabilizes the fabric, thereby virtually eliminating this concern—with one caveat: be sure to leave your foundation (if temporary) in until you have pieced your blocks together.

Though I usually use my quilters 1/4" presser foot for all quilt-related sewing, you may find an open toe foot helpful as it allows you to better see the line as you sew along.

SEWING

For paper piecing set your machine to a stitch length of 18 to 20 stitches/inch or a setting of 1½, depending on the make of your machine. The short stitch length creates a stronger stitch that won't come apart when tearing the fabric away. Also, the closely spaced perforations will facilitate tearing away the paper. Choose your thread according to the fabrics selected. Light gray is a good choice for assorted lighter fabrics, dark gray for black prints and darker fabrics.

Step-by-Step

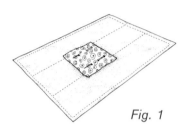

Fig. 1

Wrong side of fabric to unmarked side of foundation, held up to light to see lines for placement

1 Starting with the shape marked #1 on the pattern, place the fabric you've chosen for piece #1 with the wrong side against the unmarked side of the foundation. Hold the foundation up to a light source to help you see the marked lines. If desired, use a dab of fabric glue stick to hold the fabric piece in place. Make sure the fabric covers the shape with at least 1/4" extending over the marked line all around. Be generous with the fabric: it's better to have too big a piece than to come up short and have to tear out and start over. (Fig.1)

2 Cut a piece of fabric for piece #2. Pin piece #2 against piece #1, right sides facing. Working from the marked side of the foundation, the back, stitch along the marked line. Begin and end the stitching several stitches beyond the ends of the lines. (Fig. 2)

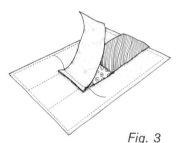

Fig. 2

Adding second piece

3 Trim the seam allowances to 1/4". For tiny pieces such as window trim, trim to 1/8".

4 Open the seam and finger press, then press with a dry iron. In the same manner, add fabric pieces #3 and so on, pressing after each piece. (Fig. 3)

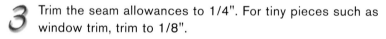

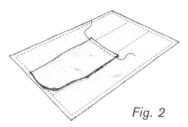

Fig. 3

Adding third piece

Tips

Use a hot dry iron, so as not to distort your block. This should also help to avoid shrinking the paper foundation and getting ink from the paper onto your iron, and inadvertently your fabric. Press only on the fabric side of the pieces.

Tips

To keep myself on track, I paper piece all sub-units (piece #1, #2, #3, etc.) and trim them. Then, before sewing them together, I lay them out by my sewing machine wrong side (marked side) up in proper finished block configuration. This way I can see clearly how they go together to form the finished block.

5 When all pieces are sewn together, lay the block fabric side down (marked foundation up) on your self-healing mat. Using a rotary cutter and ruler, trim the edges of the block piece, foundation paper and fabric along the dashed lines. This leaves a 1/4" seam allowance all the way around. (Fig. 4)

Sub-unit Blocks: Putting the Pieces Together to Form a Block

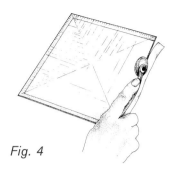

Fig. 4

Trim to 1/4" around all seams

All of the blocks in this book are comprised of sub-units, marked "piece 1 of 3, piece 2 of 3, etc." for example. To make a block, paper piece each of the sub-units, then sew them together in numeric order to form the block. Remember to press the seams open as you sew the pieces together.

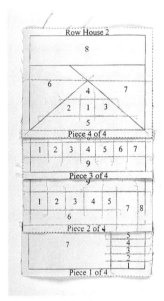

Back of block

Front of block

Tips

To avoid transferring ink from the printed paper to your ironing board cover, place a paper towel or piece of felt between the ironing board and the block.

Tips

If possible, stitch in the direction of a point. This way you can see as you come to it that you are crossing all three lines at the same point.

FINISHING YOUR QUILT
Joining Blocks

Refer to the layout diagram for the particular quilt you are making. Following the diagram, lay out the blocks and any other required fabric pieces. Sew them together to form the quilt top.

Tips

If I have any doubt that the block seams may not match perfectly, I baste them together first. Then I only have to rip out basting stitches a little to make my adjustment and re-sew with a normal stitch length.

Tips

Use vinyl-coated paper clips instead of pins to hold your pieces together for stitching. Try it!

Fig. 5

Straight cut border

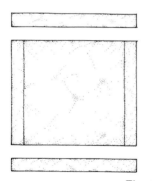

Fig. 6

Adding second set of strips for border

Adding Borders

Once you have joined the blocks, the quilt instructions may direct you to add a border. Essentially, this is a simple matter of framing the center of the quilt with strips of fabric. Cut all the pieces as required in the materials list and quilt layout diagram. Sew the first two strips to the sides of the quilt center. Press the seam allowances toward the strips. (Fig. 5)

Sew the second (longer) set of strips to the top and bottom of the quilt center. Press the seam allowances toward the strips. (Fig. 6)

Tips

Leave the paper in place until after you complete the quilt top. Blocks will be easier to align, and won't become distorted by the tearing process. Also, you needn't worry about the grain line of the block edges since the paper will stabilize them all through the construction process.

Mitered Corners

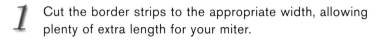

A mitered corner looks exactly like the corner of a picture frame where the two pieces of moulding are cut at a 45 degree angle, butted and nailed. Following is an easy way to do the same with fabric.

1   Cut the border strips to the appropriate width, allowing plenty of extra length for your miter.

2   Stitch the strips to the edges of the quilt top, stopping exactly 1/4" from the corners. (Fig. 7)

3   Working on one corner at a time, extend the two strips, folding and matching one as shown. Press the fold to mark it. This will form a sewing line. (Fig. 8)

4   Fold the quilt top so right sides are together. Match the border strips as shown. Stitch along the press-marked line. (Fig. 9)

5   Trim to a 1/4" seam allowance. Unfold and press. Repeat for the three remaining corners.

Removing the Paper

Now it is finally time to remove the paper from the backs of your blocks on your quilt top. To do so, gently tear the paper as if you were tearing stamps. A gentle tug against the seam will give you a head start in loosening the paper from the stitching. Press the completed quilt top gently, still using no steam. Lift the iron up and down rather than dragging it, so as not to distort the blocks.

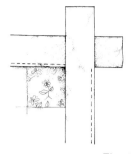

Fig. 7

*Stitch, stopping 1/4"
from corners*

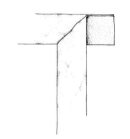

Fig. 8

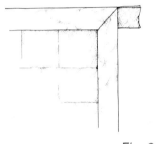

Fig. 9

Press to form sewing line

Tips

You may find a pair of tweezers helpful in the paper removal process. There are always a few pesky little tidbits of paper remaining here and there.

Three-Dimensional Appliqués

Create fun 3-D effects for your quilt with this easy appliqué method.

1 Transfer the pattern to a heavy paper or plastic. Cut it out.

2 Lay the pattern template on the wrong side of the fabric you wish to use for your appliqué. Trace around the template. (Fig. 10)

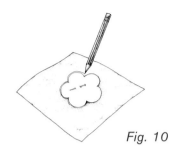

Fig. 10

3-D appliqué template

3 Lay a piece of batting down. Place a piece of the appliqué fabric on top, right side up. Lay the marked appliqué fabric on top, marked side up. Stitch along the marked line, overlapping the stitching at the beginning/end. (Fig. 11)

4 Trim the extra fabric away from the stitching, to a scant 1/4" or less. Clip the curves to the stitching where necessary. Make a slit in just the one layer of the fabric and turn the appliqué right side out through the slit. (Fig.12)

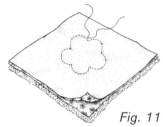

Fig. 11

Stitch to form 3-D appliqué

5 To attach the appliqués to the quilt, I use a rather large stitch by appliqué standards, and I sneak my needle in and stitch the underside of the appliqué to the quilt top. The normal method of sewing the very edges of the appliqué piece to the top would squish the 3-D effect. I refer to this as "tacking" the appliqués in place.

Basting and Quilting

Your quilt top is now ready to be made into a quilt. Mark your top for quilting before continuing on.

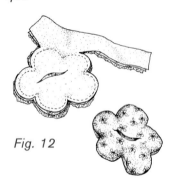

Fig. 12

Trim and turn

Quick and Easy Wallhanging Method

This no-fuss method will turn your top into a finished quilt in no time. But it is only manageable for the smallest of quilts, so I have used it for the seasonal wallhangings in this book.

1 Lay the batting on a smooth surface.

2 Lay the backing right side up on top.

3 Lay the quilt top, right side down on top of both.

Starting about 1/3 of the way from one corner of the bottom edge, stitch around the quilt top, leaving an opening at the bottom edge of the top large enough to turn the quilt right side out: about 4". (Fig. 13)

5 Trim the backing and batting even with the raw edges of the quilt top. Turn right sides out. Slipstitch the opening closed and press.

6 Quilt as desired.

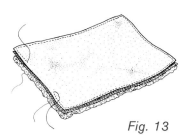

Fig. 13

Leave opening to turn

Traditional Method

1 Cut the batting and backing 3"-4" larger than the quilt top.

2 Lay the backing wrong side up on a flat surface.

3 Lay the batting on top.

4 Lay the quilt top, right side up and centered on top of the backing and batting. Working from the center out, thread or safety pin baste the three layers of the quilt "sandwich" together. (Fig. 14)

5 Quilt as desired.

6 Remove all basting stitches or any remaining safety pins.

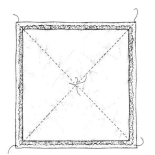

Fig. 14

Baste through all three layers of quilt "sandwich"

Tips

You may wish to try one of the new basting sprays that are on the market. These products hold the quilt layers together so you can quilt them without the use of any other form of basting. Just be sure to use the spray in a well-ventilated area. To be safe (especially since I have birds), I use any product of this type outdoors.

Binding

You may bind your quilt—finish the outside edges with fabric—by either of two methods. Self-binding is fine for smaller wall quilts. An attached binding is better for a bed quilt, considering the wear it will necessarily withstand.

Self-Binding

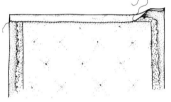

Fig. 15

Self binding, stitch sides first, then top and bottom

1 Trim the batting even with the edge of the quilt top. Trim the backing so that it's 3/4" larger than the outer edge of the quilt.

2 Along one side, fold the raw edge of the backing 1/4" to the front. Fold the backing to the front, over the edges of the batting and quilt top. Fold the sides in first and slipstitch by hand or topstitch by machine. (Fig. 15)

3 Repeat at the top and bottom.

Attached Binding

The width of your binding depends upon the size of your quilt. For a wallhanging-size quilt, the finished binding (front of quilt) should be about 1/4". The larger size bed quilt requires a binding of 1/2" on the front of the quilt. As an easy rule of thumb, cut your binding strips 1¾" for wallhangings and 3¼" for bed quilts.

1 Trim the batting and backing so that they are even with the quilt top.

2 To determine how long a binding to make, add the measurements of the four sides of your quilt top and add an extra 8".

3 Cut strips of fabric for binding along the straight, crosswise grain (there is some give to the crosswise grain) of your fabric. Use a diagonal seam to piece the strips together if necessary. (Fig. 16)

4 Wrong sides together, fold the seamed strips lengthwise in half. Press. (Fig. 17)

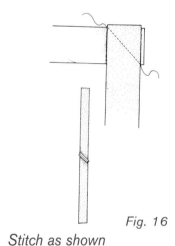

Fig. 16

Stitch as shown

Fig. 17

Attached binding

5 On the right side with raw edges even, place the binding strip along one edge of the quilt top. Using a 1/4" seam allowance, machine-stitch the binding to the quilt "sandwich." Leave the first 3" or so of the binding unstitched so you can join the two ends of the binding later.

6 At the first corner, stop stitching 1/4" from the edge of the quilt. Raise the presser foot, but leave the needle down in the fabric. (Fig. 18)

7 Pivot, and stitch diagonally to the corner of the quilt and off. (Fig. 19)

8 Hold the binding so the loose end is straight up from the next side. (Fig. 20)

9 Fold the loose binding down, matching the raw edge to that of the next side of the quilt, and sew to the next corner. (Fig. 21) Repeat for the remaining corners.

10 When you approach about 4" of the beginning of the binding, stop stitching. Match the ends of the binding as shown, opening them up to stitch them together along the diagonal. (Fig. 22)

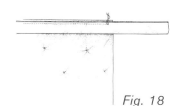
Fig. 18
Stitch, leaving corner of binding free to turn

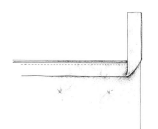
Fig. 19
Pivot and stitch to corner

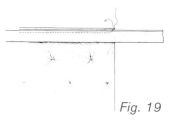
Fold binding so   *Fig. 20*
side remains free to turn

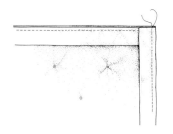
Match raw edges   *Fig. 21*
and continue stitching

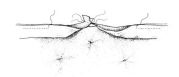
Fig. 22
Match ends and stitch closed before finishing

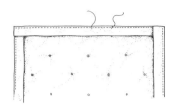

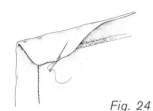

Fig. 23

Finish sewing

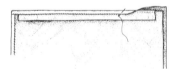

Fig. 24

Fold binding to back of quilt and stitch

11 Refold and finish sewing the seam. (Fig. 23)

12 Fold the binding to the back of the quilt over the raw edges of the quilt "sandwich," covering the machine stitching at the back of the quilt. Slipstitch the binding in place. (Fig. 24)

Adding a Hanging Sleeve

1 To hang a quilt on a wall, sew a simple sleeve to the back. A rod or 3/8" to 3/4" dowel slipped into the sleeve provides the support to hang your quilt nicely. Cut the dowel 1" longer than the sleeve.

2 Cut a strip of fabric 3½" wide and as long as the width of your quilt less 1" to 2". Press each short end 1/4" to the wrong side twice. Topstitch. (Fig. 25)

3 Wrong sides together, fold the sleeve strip lengthwise in half. Center the raw edge of the strip along the top edge of the back of the quilt before attaching the binding. Baste.

Stitch the binding to the quilt as instructed above, securing the sleeve in the seam. (Fig. 26) Slipstitch the bottom, folded edge of the sleeve to the back of the quilt.

Fig. 25

Finishing edges of sleeve

Fig. 26

Enclose sewn edge inside binding and stitch

The Block Designs

House 1

Finished size 10" x 8"

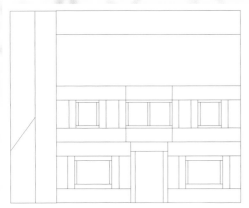

Note: The piecing diagram and pattern pieces are mirror images of the sewn block.

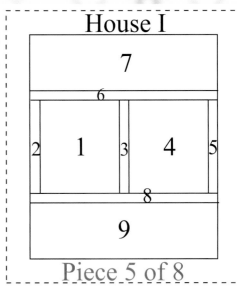

Note: The order for sewing the fabric to the pattern pieces is shown in black. The piecing sequence (1 of 5, 2 of 5, etc.) showing the order to sew the pattern pieces to form the finished block is shown in red.

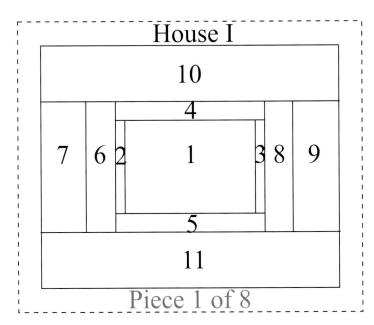

House I

10

4

7 6 2 1 3 8 9

5

11

Piece 1 of 8

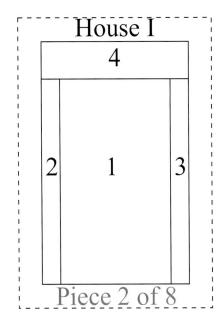

House I

4

2 1 3

Piece 2 of 8

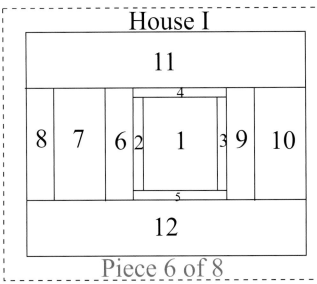

House I

11

8 7 6 2 1 3 9 10

5

12

Piece 6 of 8

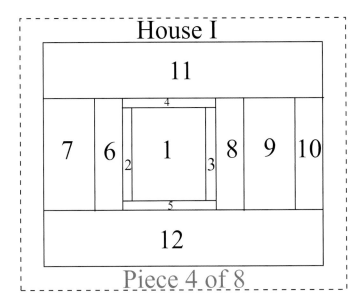

House I

11

7 6 2 1 3 8 9 10

5

12

Piece 4 of 8

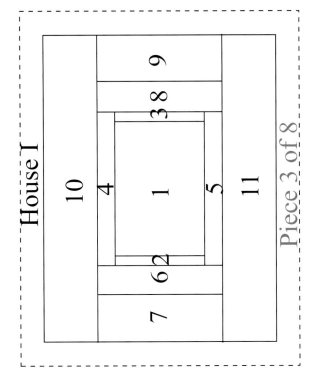

House I

10

4

3 8 9

1

6 2 5

7

11

Piece 3 of 8

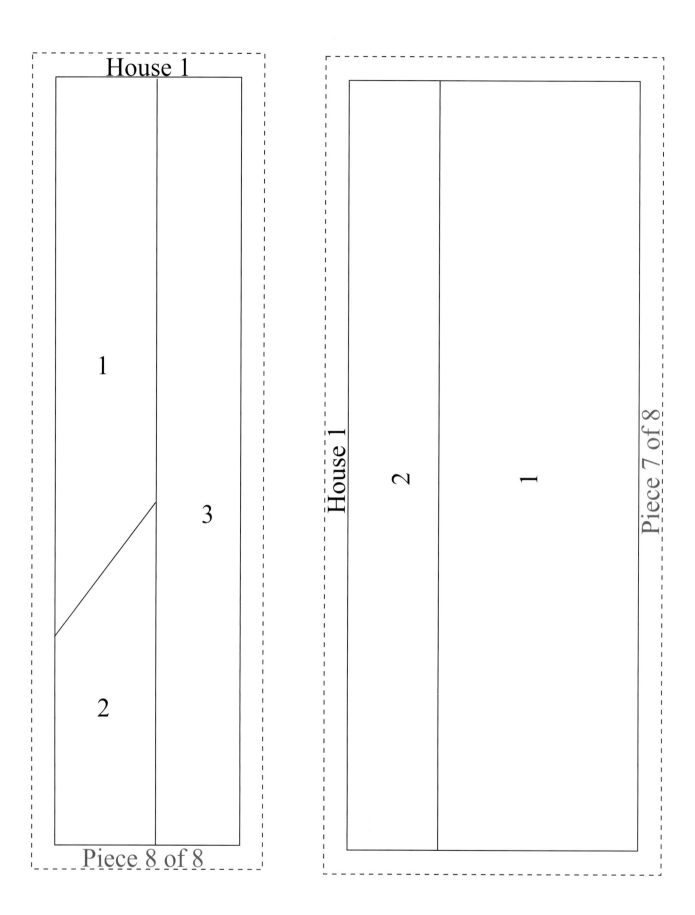

House 1

1

3

2

Piece 8 of 8

House 1

2

1

Piece 7 of 8

22

House 2

Finished size 10" x 8"

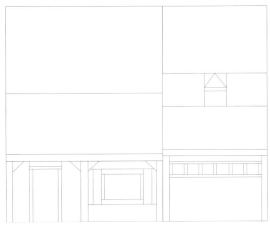

Note: The piecing diagram and pattern pieces are mirror images of the sewn block.

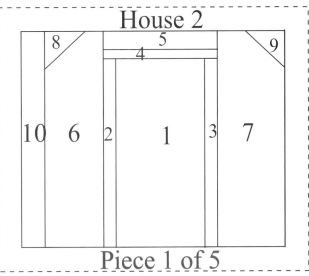

House 2

Piece 1 of 5

Note: The order for sewing the fabric to the pattern pieces is shown in black. The piecing sequence (1 of 5, 2 of 5, etc.) showing the order to sew the pattern pieces to form the finished block is shown in red.

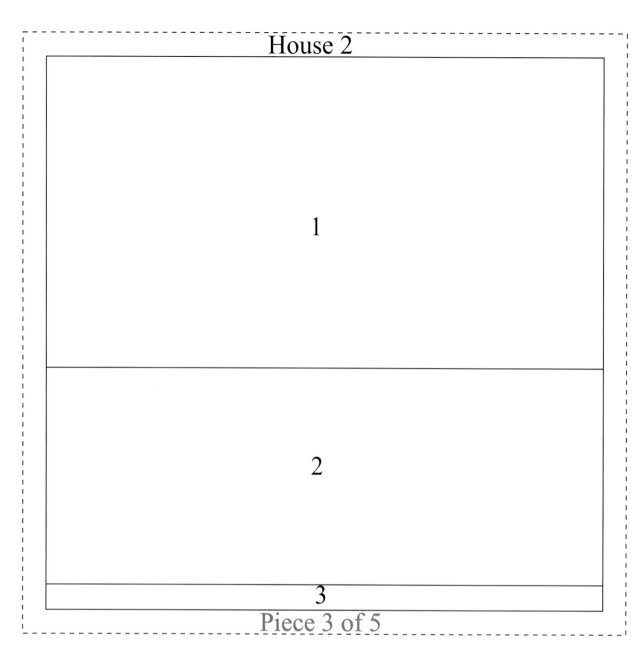

1

2

3

Piece 3 of 5

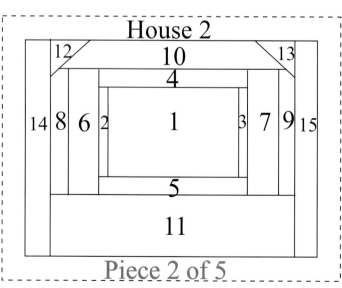

House 2

12 10 13
4
14 8 6 2 1 3 7 9 15
5
11

Piece 2 of 5

24

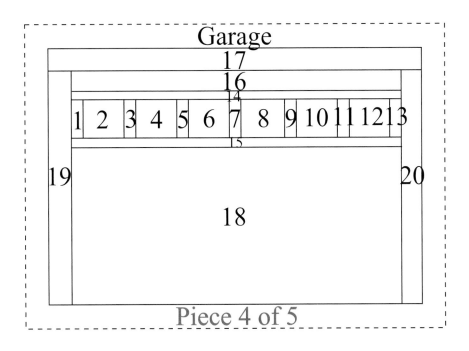

Garage

17
16
14

| 1 | 2 | 3 | 4 | 5 | 6 | 7 | 8 | 9 | 10 | 11 | 12 | 13 |

15

19

20

18

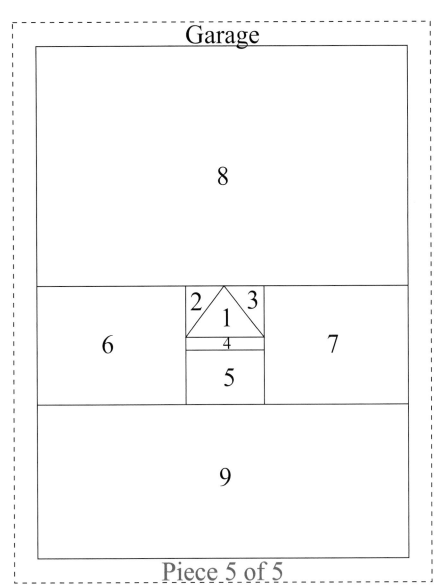

Garage

8

2 △ 3
1
6   4   7
5

9

House 3

Finished size 10" x 8"

Note: The piecing diagram and pattern pieces are mirror images of the sewn block.

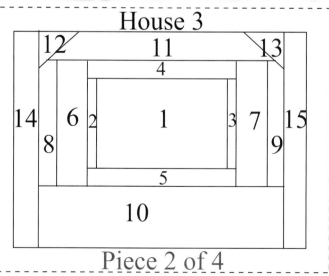

House 3

Piece 2 of 4

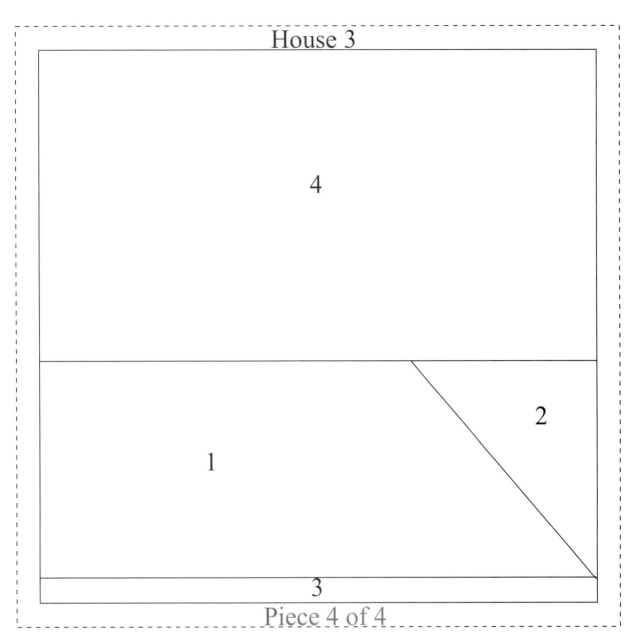

Piece 4 of 4

Note: The order for sewing the fabric to the pattern pieces is shown in black. The piecing sequence (1 of 5, 2 of 5, etc.) showing the order to sew the pattern pieces to form the finished block is shown in red.

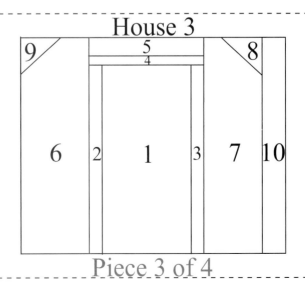

House 3

Piece 3 of 4

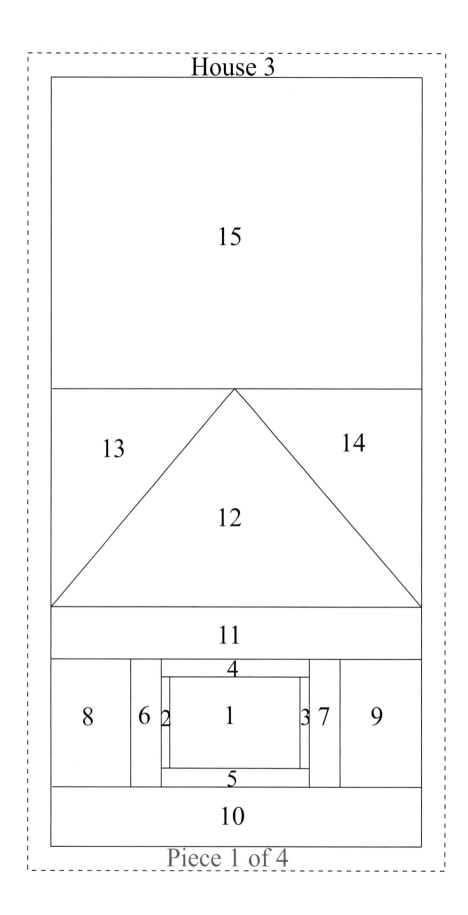

House 3

15

13   14

12

11

4

8   6 2   1   3 7   9

5

10

House 4

Finished size 10" x 8"

Note: The piecing diagram and pattern pieces are mirror images of the sewn block.

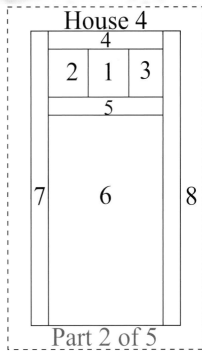

House 4

4		
2	1	3

5

| 7 | 6 | 8 |

Part 2 of 5

Note: The order for sewing the fabric to the pattern pieces is shown in black. The piecing sequence (1 of 5, 2 of 5, etc.) showing the order to sew the pattern pieces to form the finished block is shown in red.

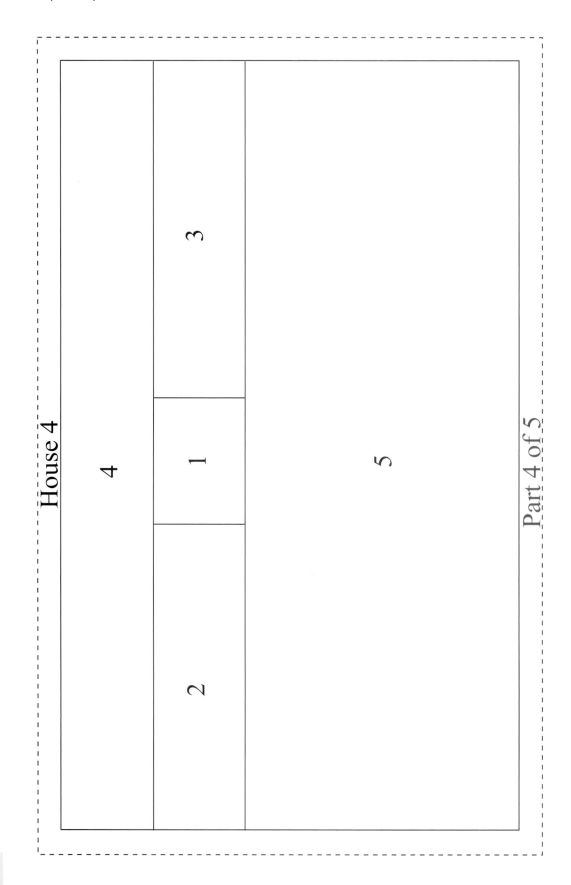

House 4

Part 4 of 5

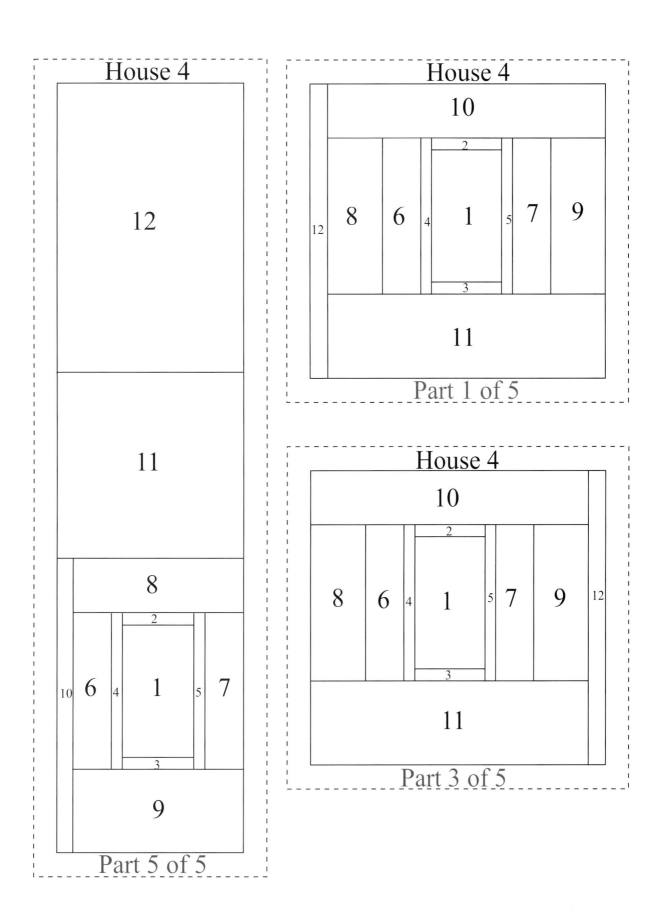

House 5

Finished size 10" x 8"

Note: The piecing diagram and pattern pieces are mirror images of the sewn block.

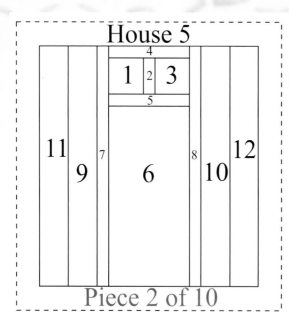

House 5

Piece 2 of 10

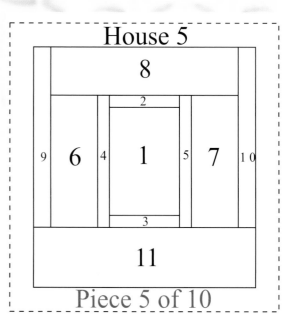

House 5

Piece 5 of 10

Note: The order for sewing the fabric to the pattern pieces is shown in black. The piecing sequence (1 of 5, 2 of 5, etc.) showing the order to sew the pattern pieces to form the finished block is shown in red.

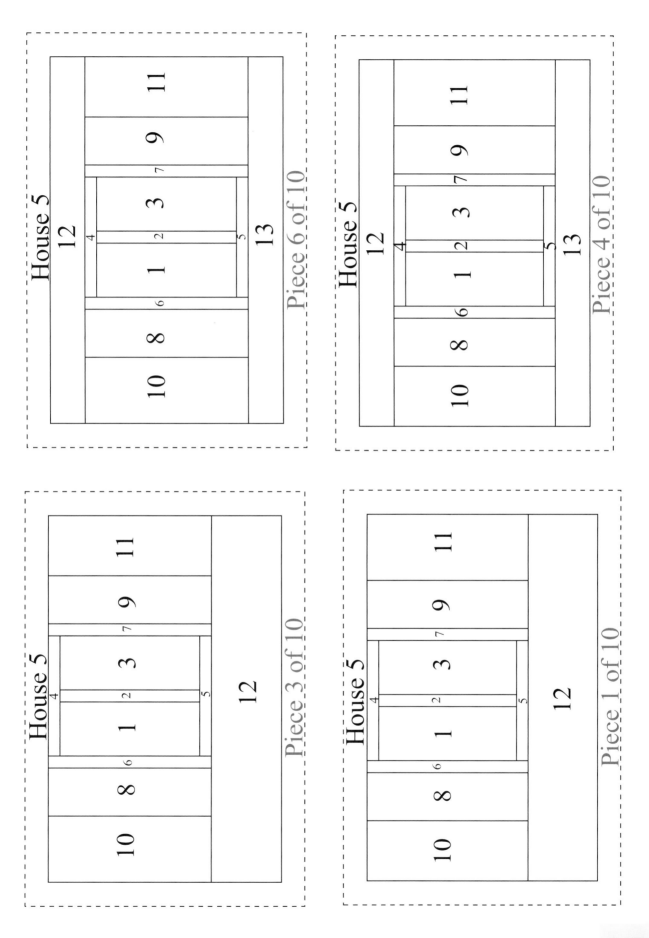

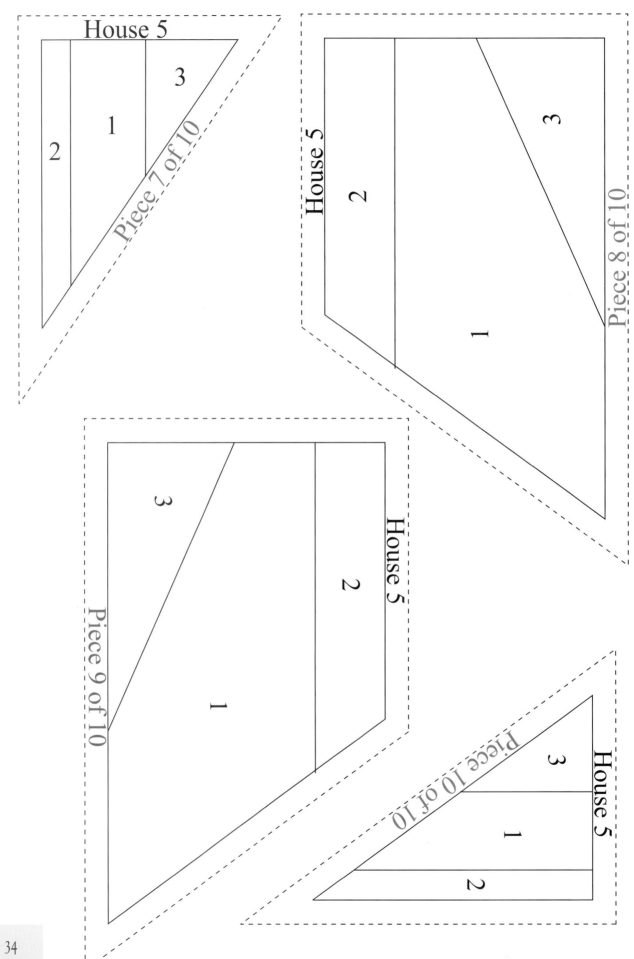

House 5

Piece 7 of 10

3
1
2

House 5

Piece 8 of 10

3
2
1

House 5

Piece 9 of 10

3
2
1

House 5

Piece 10 of 10

3
1
2

House 6

Finished size 10" x 8"

Note: The piecing diagram and pattern pieces are mirror images of the sewn block.

Note: The order for sewing the fabric to the pattern pieces is shown in black. The piecing sequence (1 of 5, 2 of 5, etc.) showing the order to sew the pattern pieces to form the finished block is shown in red.

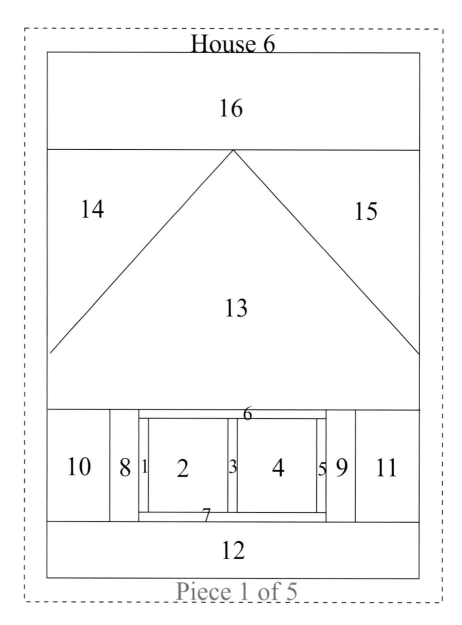

House 6

16

14   15

13

10   8 1   2   3   4   5 9   11

6

7

12

Piece 1 of 5

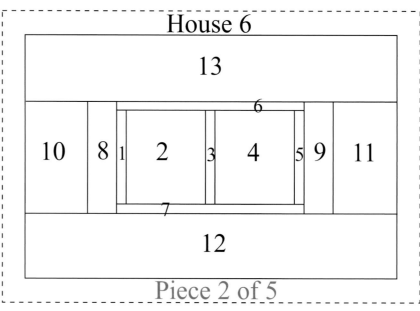

House 6

13

10   8 1   2   3   4   5 9   11

6

7

12

Piece 2 of 5

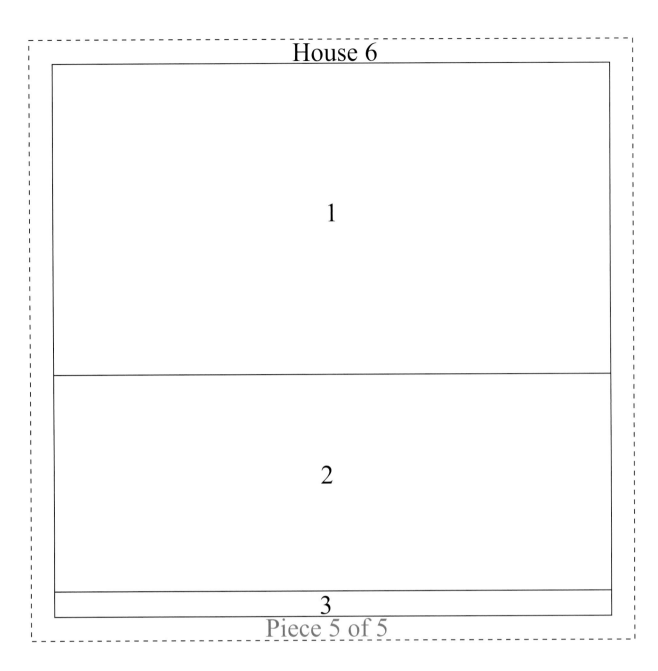

1

2

3

Piece 5 of 5

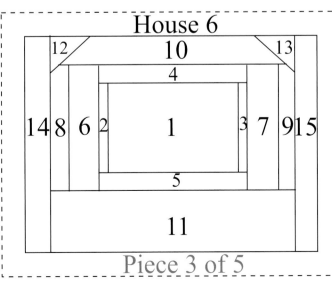

12   10   13
4
14 8 6 2   1   3 7 9 15
5
11

Piece 3 of 5

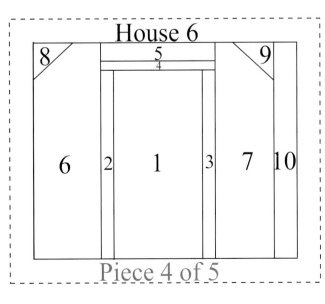

8   5   9
4
6   2   1   3   7 10

Piece 4 of 5

House 7

Finished size 10" x 8"

Note: The piecing diagram and pattern pieces
are mirror images of the sewn block.

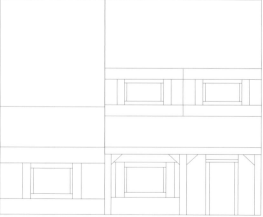

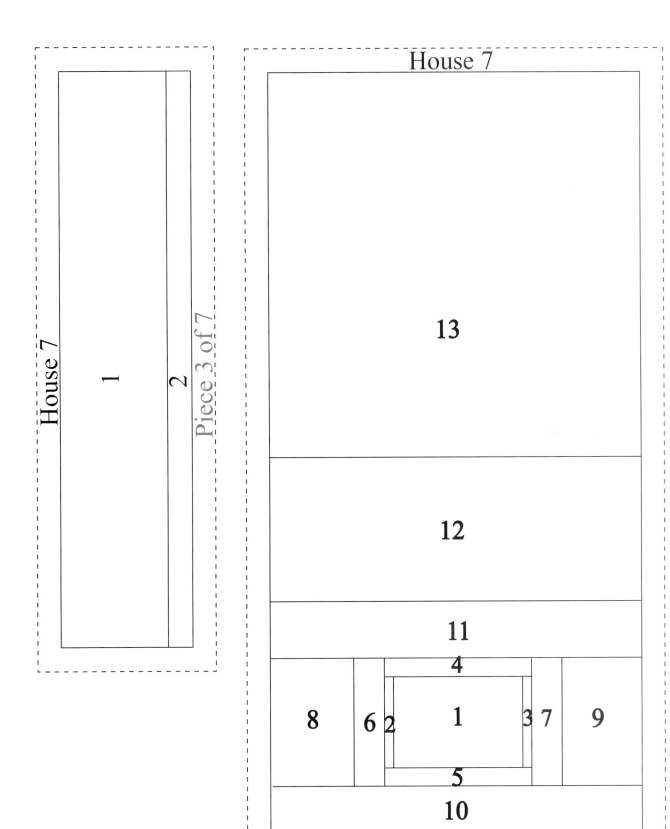

House 7

1

2

Piece 3 of 7

13

12

11

4

8   6 2   1   3 7   9

5

10

Piece 7 of 7

Note: The order for sewing the fabric to the pattern pieces is shown in black. The piecing sequence (1 of 5, 2 of 5, etc.) showing the order to sew the pattern pieces to form the finished block is shown in red.

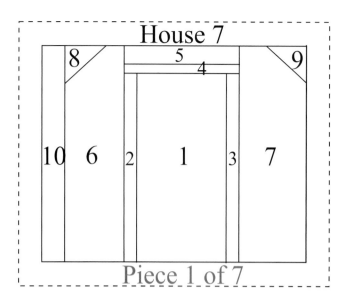

Piece 1 of 7

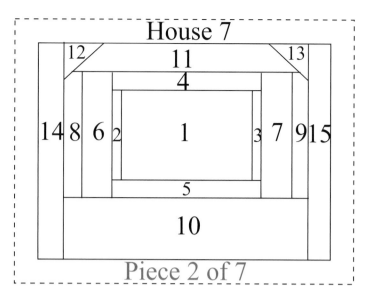

Piece 2 of 7

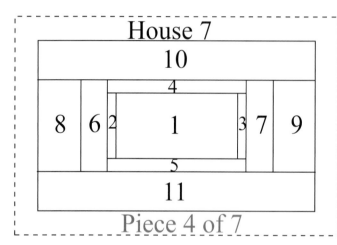

Piece 4 of 7

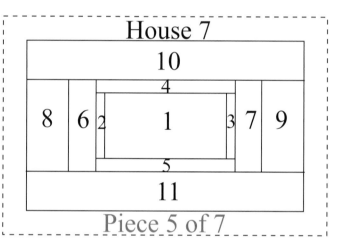

Piece 5 of 7

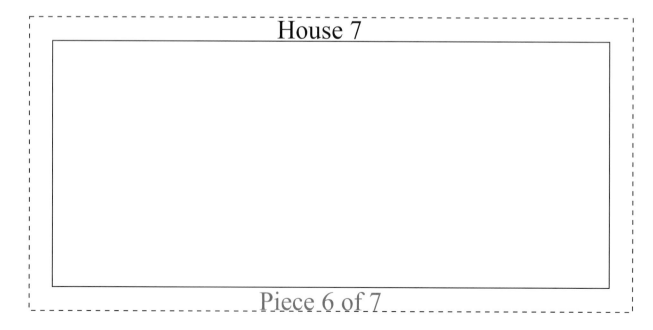

Piece 6 of 7

Small Victorian House

Finished size 6" x 4"

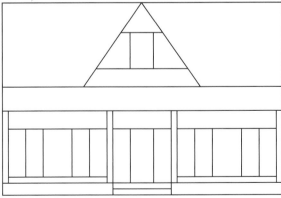

Note: The piecing diagram and pattern pieces are mirror images of the sewn block.

Victorian House

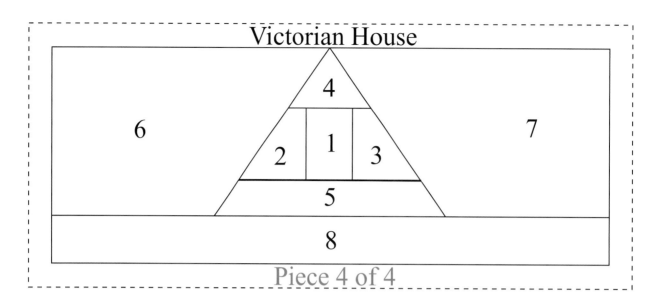

Piece 4 of 4

Victorian House

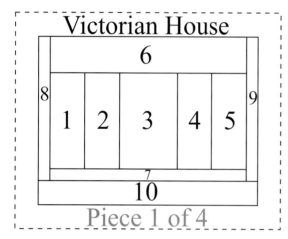

Piece 1 of 4

Victorian House

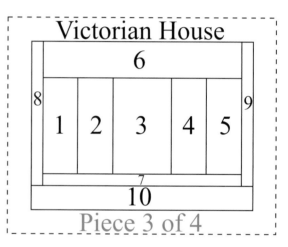

Piece 3 of 4

Victorian House

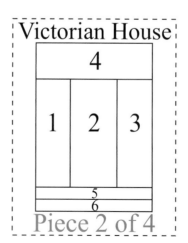

Piece 2 of 4

Note: The order for sewing the fabric to the pattern pieces is shown in black. The piecing sequence (1 of 5, 2 of 5, etc.) showing the order to sew the pattern pieces to form the finished block is shown in red.

Large Victorian House

Finished size 8" x 8"

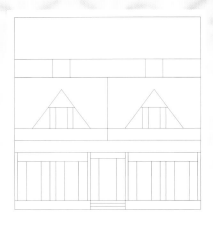

Note: The piecing diagram and pattern pieces are mirror images of the sewn block.

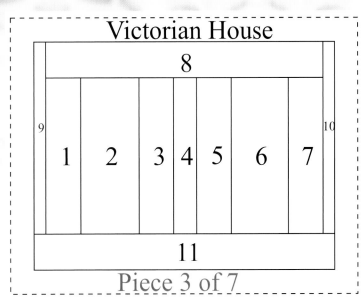

Victorian House

8						
1	2	3	4	5	6	7

9

10

11

Piece 3 of 7

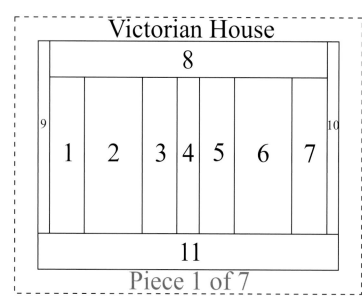

Victorian House

Piece 1 of 7

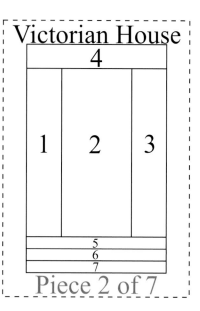

Victorian House

Piece 2 of 7

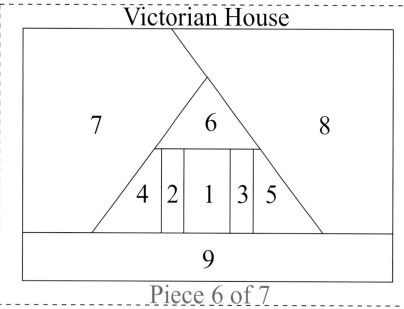

Victorian House

Piece 6 of 7

Note: The order for sewing the fabric to the pattern pieces is shown in black. The piecing sequence (1 of 5, 2 of 5, etc.) showing the order to sew the pattern pieces to form the finished block is shown in red.

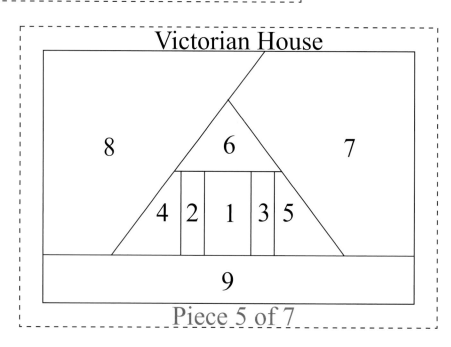

Victorian House

Piece 5 of 7

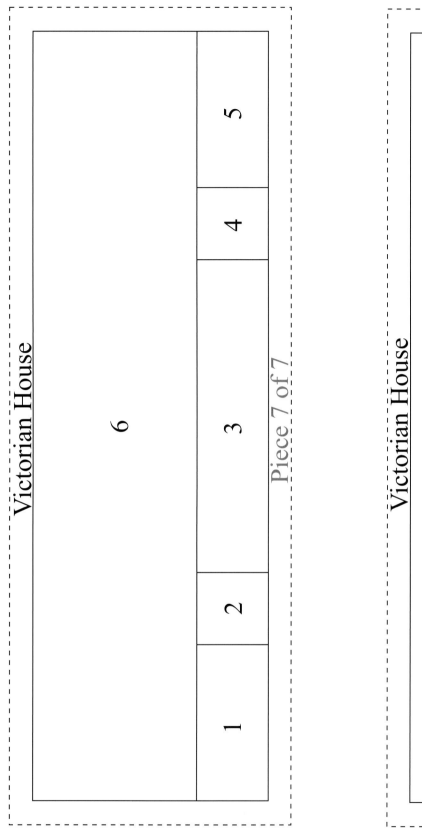

Victorian House

6

3

4

5

1

2

Victorian House

Cape Cod House

Finished size 10" x 8"

Note: The piecing diagram and pattern pieces are mirror images of the sewn block.

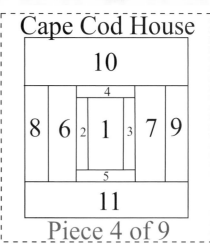

Cape Cod House

				10				
				4				
8	6	2	1		3	7	9	
				5				
				11				

Piece 4 of 9

Note: The order for sewing the fabric to the pattern pieces is shown in black. The piecing sequence (1 of 5, 2 of 5, etc.) showing the order to sew the pattern pieces to form the finished block is shown in red.

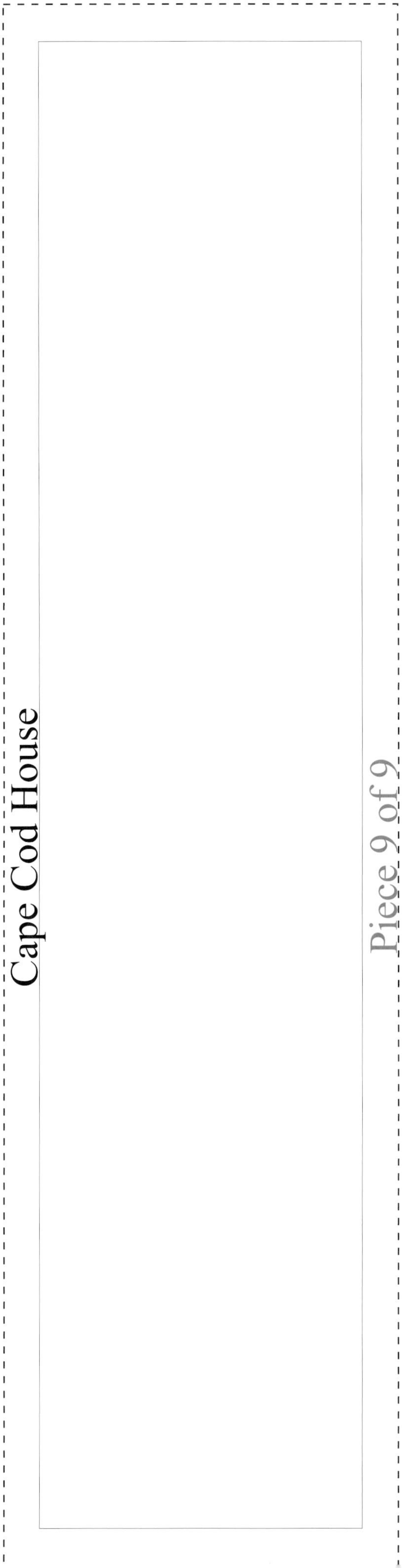
Cape Cod House
Piece 9 of 9

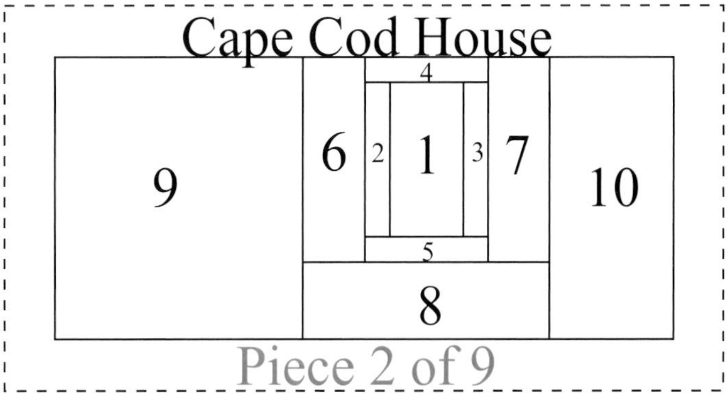
Cape Cod House
9
6
2
1
3
7
10
4
5
8
Piece 2 of 9

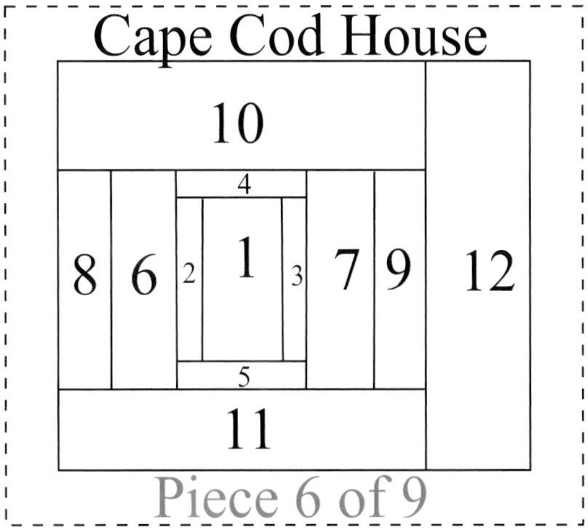
Cape Cod House
10
4
8
6
2
1
3
7
9
12
5
11
Piece 6 of 9

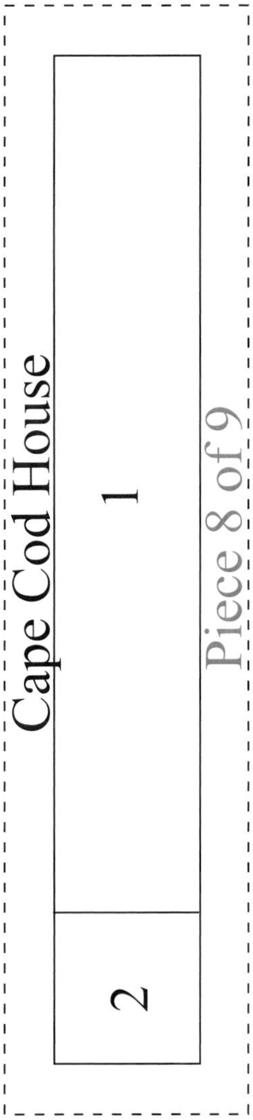
Cape Cod House
1
2
Piece 8 of 9

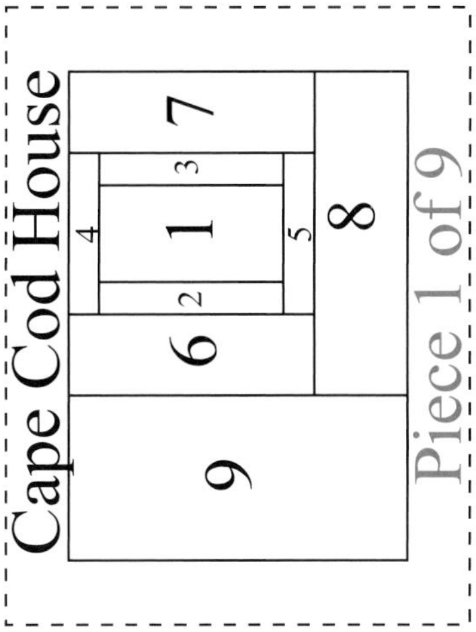
Cape Cod House
7
3
4
1
5
8
2
6
9
Piece 1 of 9

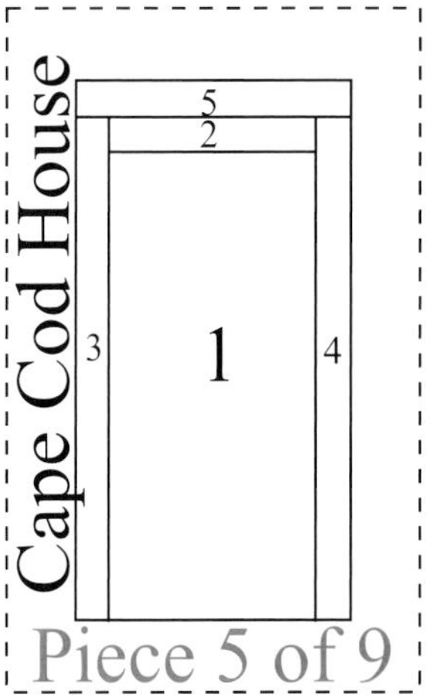
Cape Cod House
5
2
3
1
4
Piece 5 of 9

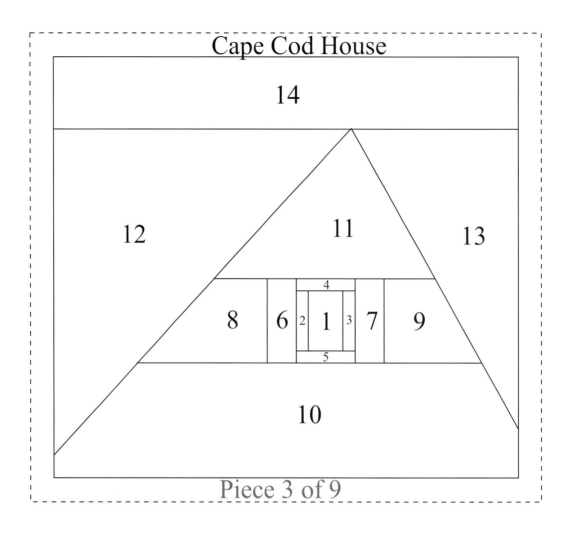

Cape Cod House

Piece 3 of 9

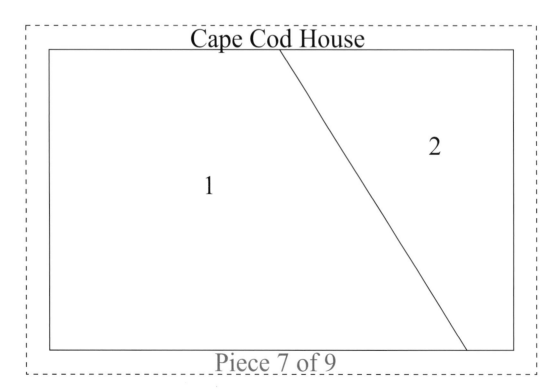

Cape Cod House

Piece 7 of 9

Church

Finished size 10" x 10"

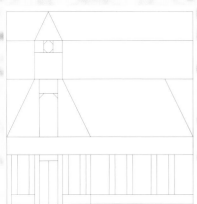

Note: The piecing diagram and pattern pieces are mirror images of the sewn block.

Note: The order for sewing the fabric to the pattern pieces is shown in black. The piecing sequence (1 of 5, 2 of 5, etc.) showing the order to sew the pattern pieces to form the finished block is shown in red.

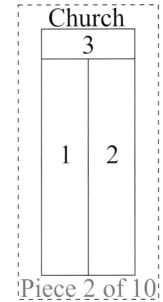

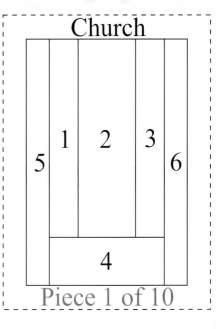

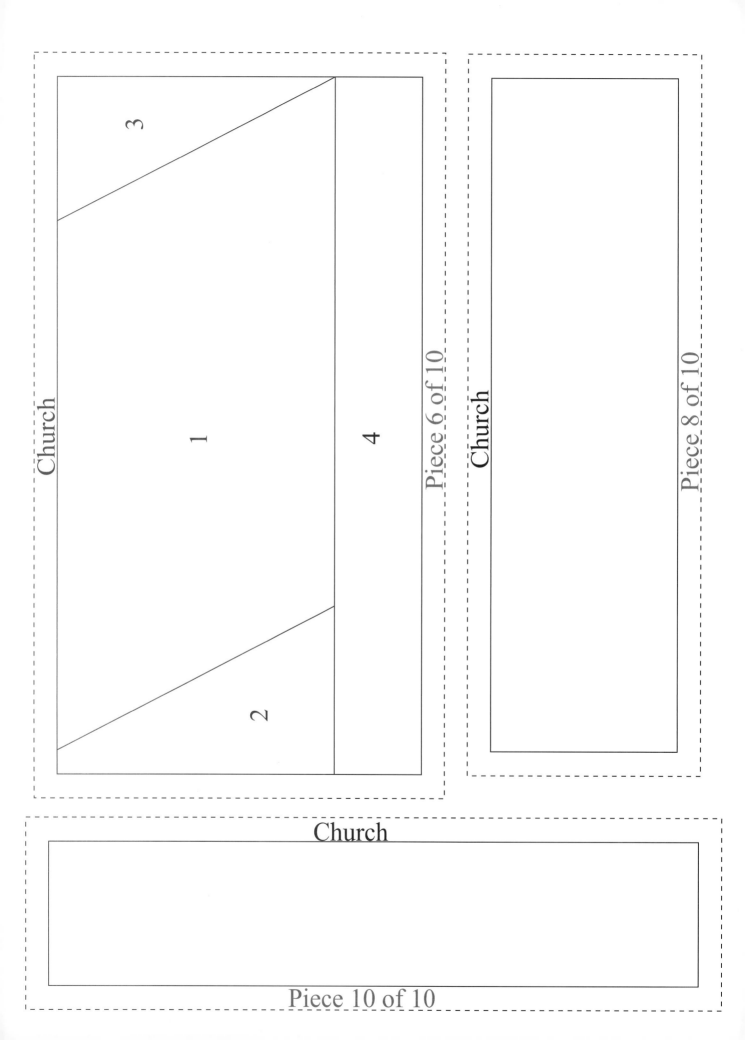

Church

3

1

2

4

Church

Church

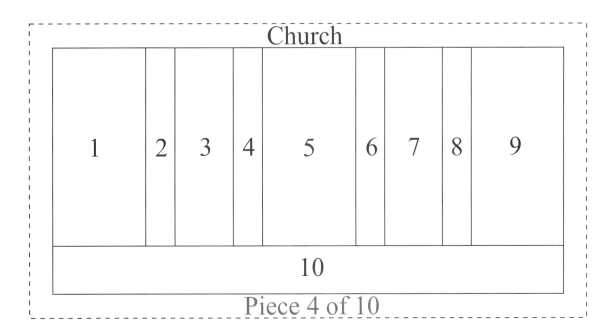

Church

1 2 3 4 5 6 7 8 9

10

Piece 4 of 10

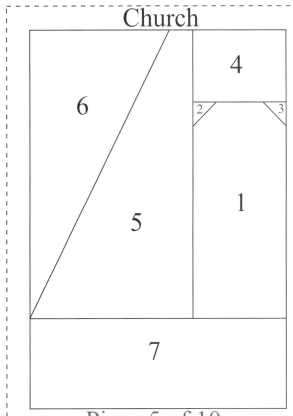

Church

6
4
2 3
5
1
7

Piece 5 of 10

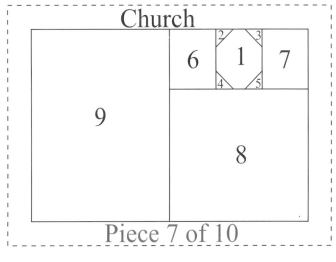

Church

6 1 7
2 3
4 5
9
8

Piece 7 of 10

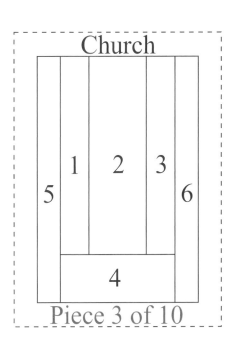

Church

5 1 2 3 6
4

Piece 3 of 10

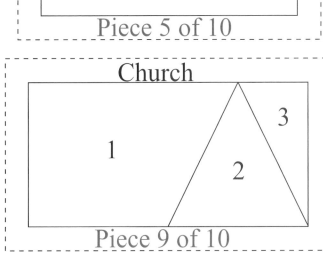

Church

1
3
2

Piece 9 of 10

Schoolhouse

Finished size 10" x 8"

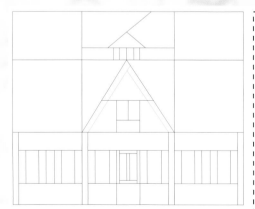

Note: The piecing diagram and pattern pieces are mirror images of the sewn block.

Note: The order for sewing the fabric to the pattern pieces is shown in black. The piecing sequence (1 of 5, 2 of 5, etc.) showing the order to sew the pattern pieces to form the finished block is shown in red.

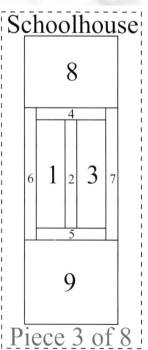

Schoolhouse

Piece 3 of 8

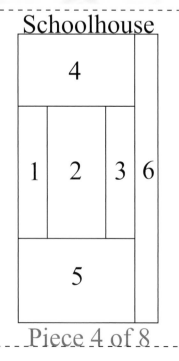

Schoolhouse

Piece 4 of 8

52

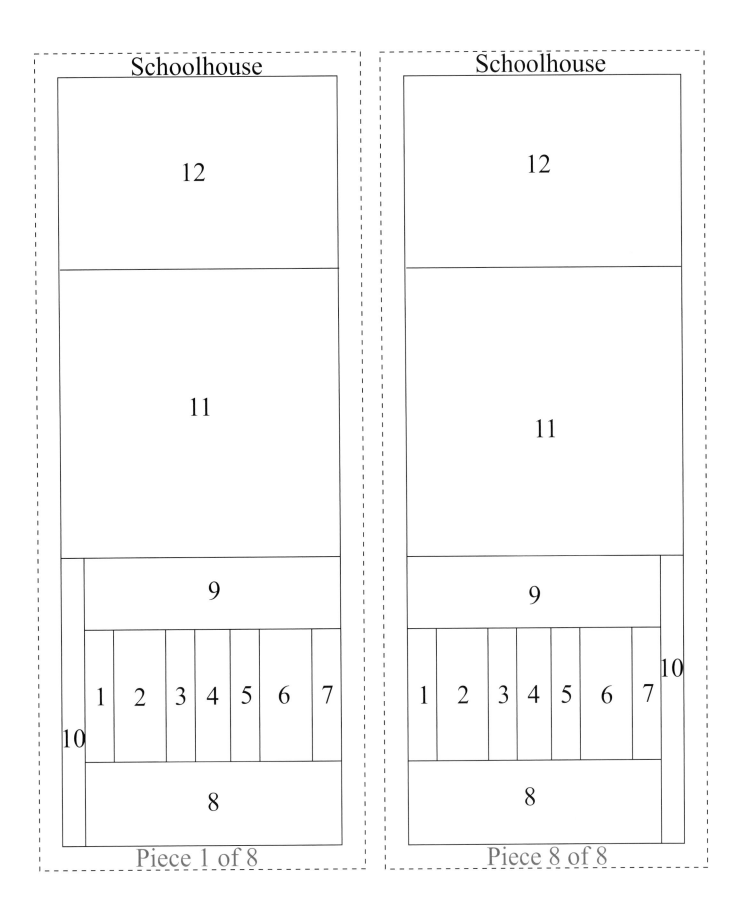

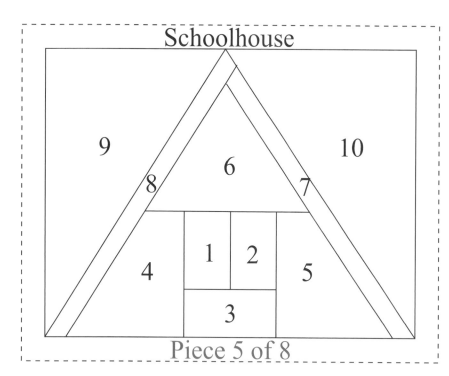

Schoolhouse

9   10

8   6   7

1   2

4   3   5

Piece 5 of 8

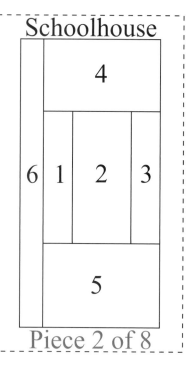

Schoolhouse

4

6 1 2 3

5

Piece 2 of 8

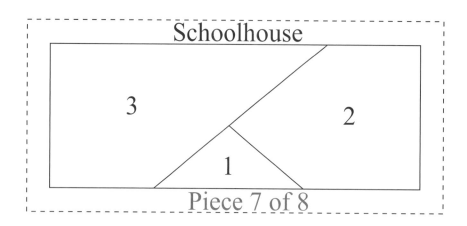

Schoolhouse

3   2

1

Piece 7 of 8

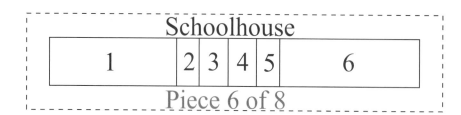

Schoolhouse

1   2 3 4 5   6

Piece 6 of 8

Barn

Finished size 12" x 8"

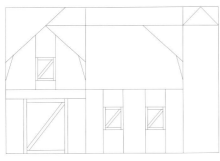

Note: The piecing diagram and pattern pieces are mirror images of the sewn block.

Note: The order for sewing the fabric to the pattern pieces is shown in black. The piecing sequence (1 of 5, 2 of 5, etc.) showing the order to sew the pattern pieces to form the finished block is shown in red.

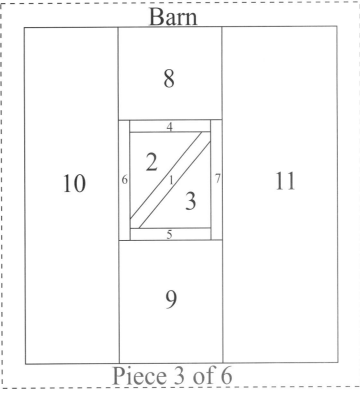

Barn

Piece 3 of 6

Barn

3   4
2

1

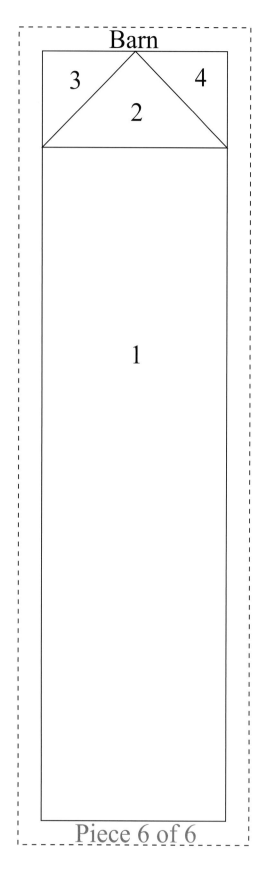

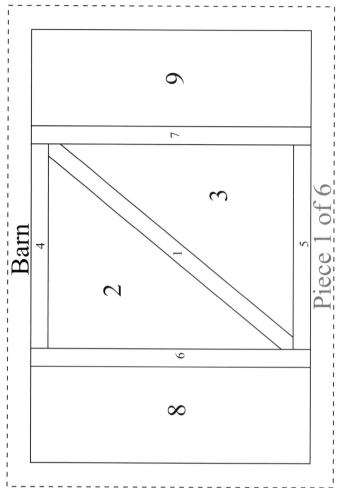

9

7

Barn

4

3

2

1

5

6

8

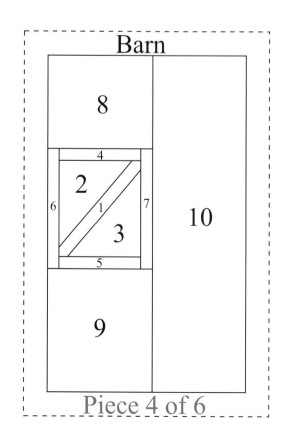

Barn

8

4
2
6   7
1
3
5

10

9

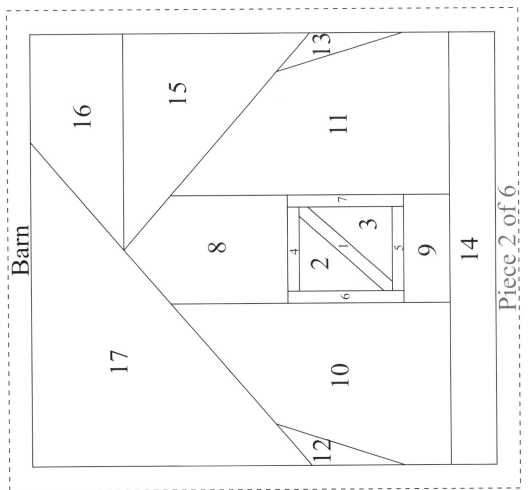

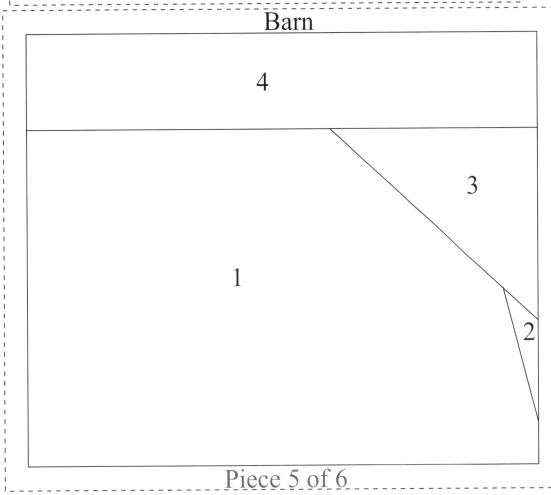

Row House 1

Finished size 4" x 8"

Note: The piecing diagram and pattern pieces are mirror images of the sewn block.

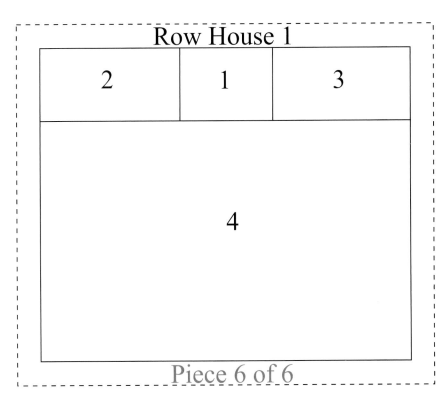

Row House 1

Piece 6 of 6

Note: The order for sewing the fabric to the pattern pieces is shown in black. The piecing sequence (1 of 5, 2 of 5, etc.) showing the order to sew the pattern pieces to form the finished block is shown in red.

Row House 1

1	2	3
4		

Piece 2 of 6

Row House 1

1	2	3
4		

Piece 4 of 6

Row House 1

8						
1	2	3	4	5	6	7
9						

Piece 5 of 6

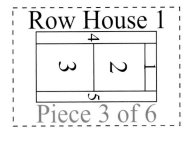

Row House 1

Piece 3 of 6

Row House 1

6	1	7
	2	
	3	
	4	
	5	

Piece 1 of 6

Row House 2

Finished size 4" x 8"

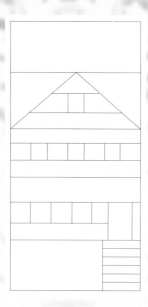

Note: The piecing diagram and pattern pieces are mirror images of the sewn block.

Note: Fabric pieces #6 and #7 of sub-unit piece 4 can be made of sky fabric to match the fabric piece #8, or of a different fabric to resemble a roof.

Note: The order for sewing the fabric to the pattern pieces is shown in black. The piecing sequence (1 of 5, 2 of 5, etc.) showing the order to sew the pattern pieces to form the finished block is shown in red.

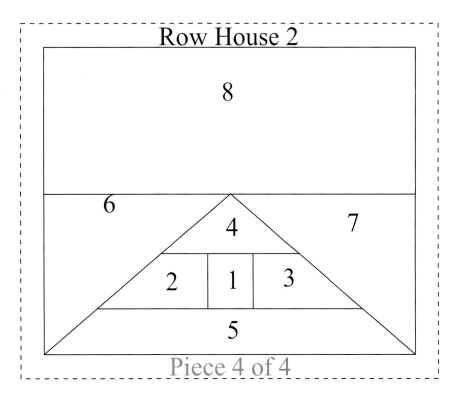

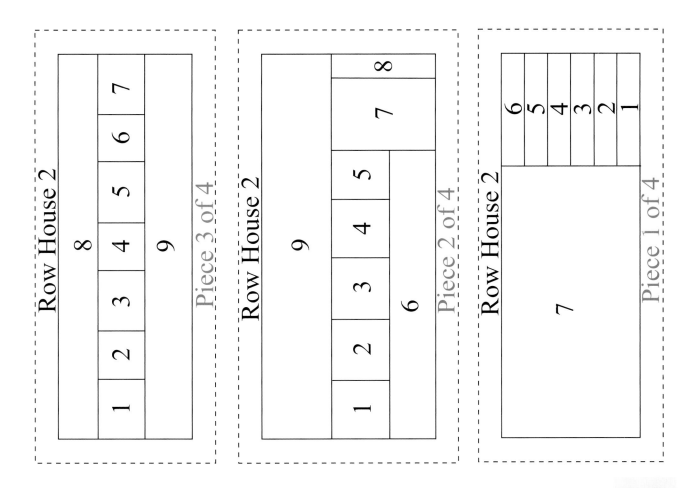

Row House 3

Finished size 4" x 8"

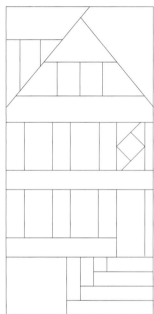

Note: The piecing diagram and pattern pieces are mirror images of the sewn block.

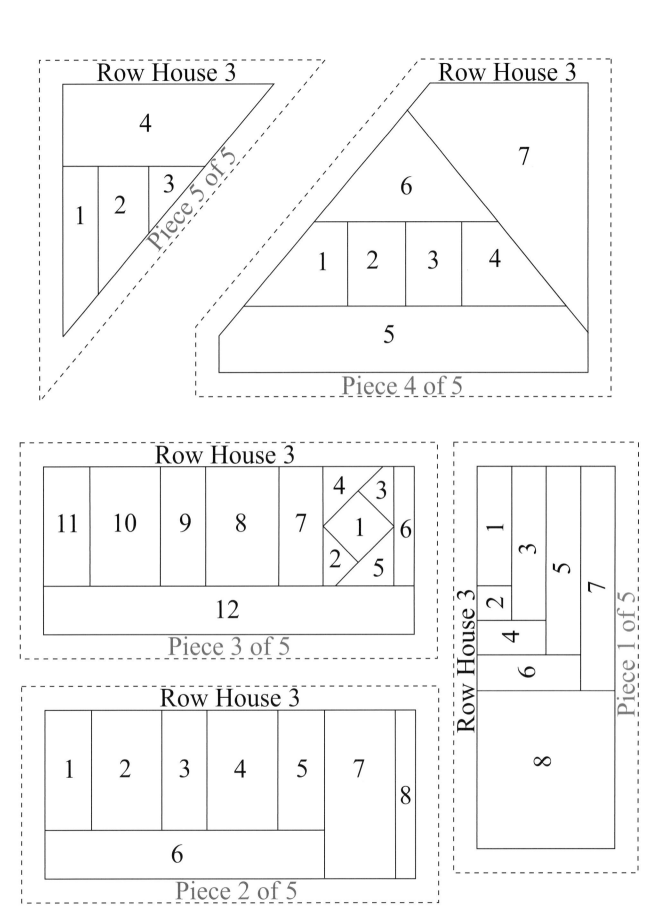

Note: The order for sewing the fabric to the pattern pieces is shown in black. The piecing sequence (1 of 5, 2 of 5, etc.) showing the order to sew the pattern pieces to form the finished block is shown in red.

Row House 4

Finished size 4" x 8"

Note: The piecing diagram and pattern pieces are mirror images of the sewn block.

Note: The order for sewing the fabric to the pattern pieces is shown in black. The piecing sequence (1 of 5, 2 of 5, etc.) showing the order to sew the pattern pieces to form the finished block is shown in red.

Row House 4

6	5	7
	4	
	3	
	2	
	1	

Piece 1 of 8

Row House 4

6

| 1 | 2 | 3 | 4 | 5 |

7

Piece 8 of 8

Row House 4

13

| 8 | 7 | 6 | 5 | 3 / 1 | 2 / 4 | 9 | 10 | 11 | 12 |

14

Piece 5 of 8

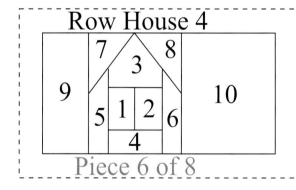

Row House 4

Piece 6 of 8

Row House 4

| 1 | 2 |

3

Piece 3 of 8

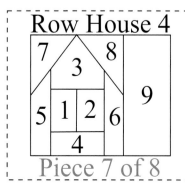

Row House 4

Piece 7 of 8

Row House 4

| 1 | 2 | 3 | 4 |

5

Piece 4 of 8

Row House 4

| 1 | 2 | 3 | 4 |

5

Piece 2 of 8

Rail Fence

Finished size 10" x 1 1/2"

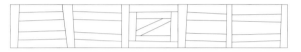

Note: The piecing diagram and pattern pieces are mirror images of the sewn block.

Rail Fence

Piece 1 of 5

Rail Fence

Piece 4 of 5

Rail Fence

Piece 5 of 5

Rail Fence

Piece 2 of 5

Note: The order for sewing the fabric to the pattern pieces is shown in black. The piecing sequence (1 of 5, 2 of 5, etc.) showing the order to sew the pattern pieces to form the finished block is shown in red.

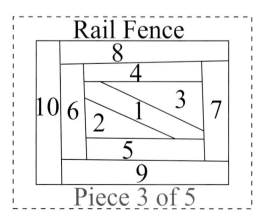

Rail Fence

Piece 3 of 5

Picket Fence

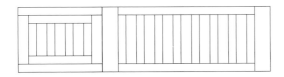

Note: The piecing diagram and pattern pieces are mirror images of the sewn block.

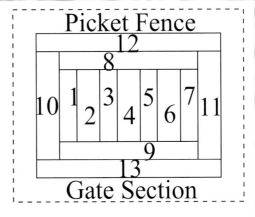

Picket Fence

Gate Section

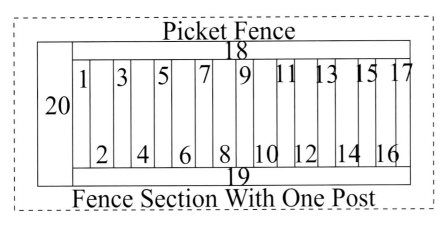

Picket Fence

Fence Section With One Post

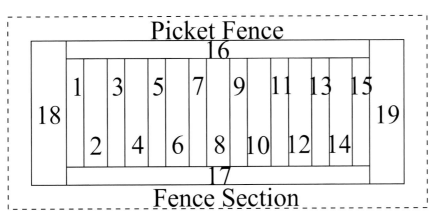

Picket Fence

Fence Section

Log Cabin

Finished size 8" x 8"

Note: The piecing diagram and pattern pieces are mirror images of the sewn block.

Log Cabin

6

5

4

3

2

1

Piece 10 of 11

Log Cabin

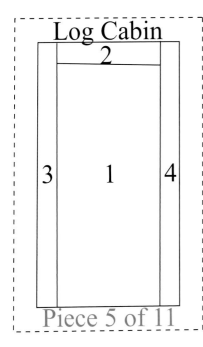

2

3   1   4

Piece 5 of 11

Log Cabin

5

2   1   3

4

Piece 2 of 11

Log Cabin

6

5

4

3

2

1

Piece 3 of 11

Note: The order for sewing the fabric to the pattern pieces is shown in black. The piecing sequence (1 of 5, 2 of 5, etc.) showing the order to sew the pattern pieces to form the finished block is shown in red.

69

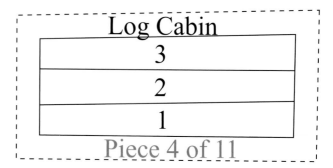

Log Cabin

| 3 |
| 2 |
| 1 |

Piece 4 of 11

Log Cabin

| 3 |
| 2 |
| 1 |

Piece 9 of 11

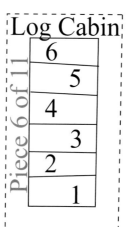

Log Cabin

Piece 6 of 11

| 6 |
| 5 |
| 4 |
| 3 |
| 2 |
| 1 |

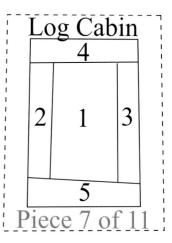

Log Cabin

	4	
2	1	3
	5	

Piece 7 of 11

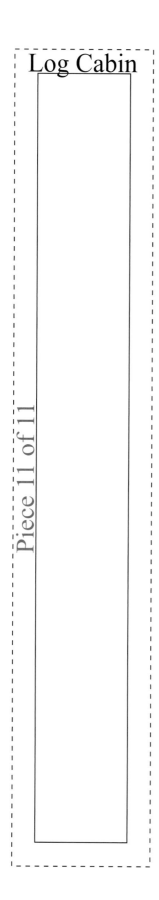

Log Cabin

Piece 11 of 11

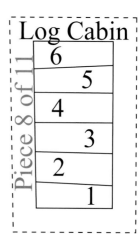

Log Cabin

Piece 1 of 11

| 6 |
| 5 |
| 4 |
| 3 |
| 2 |
| 1 |

Log Cabin

Piece 8 of 11

| 6 |
| 5 |
| 4 |
| 3 |
| 2 |
| 1 |

Light House

Finished size 4" x 12"

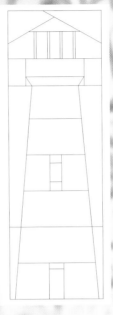

Note: The piecing diagram and pattern pieces are mirror images of the sewn block.

Note: The order for sewing the fabric to the pattern pieces is shown in black. The piecing sequence (1 of 5, 2 of 5, etc.) showing the order to sew the pattern pieces to form the finished block is shown in red.

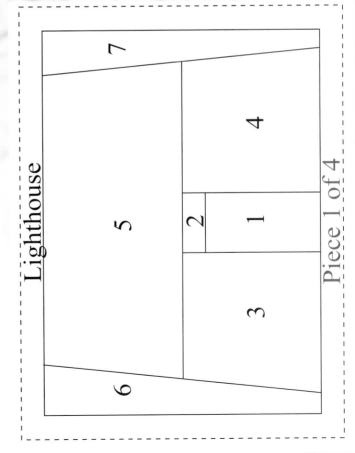

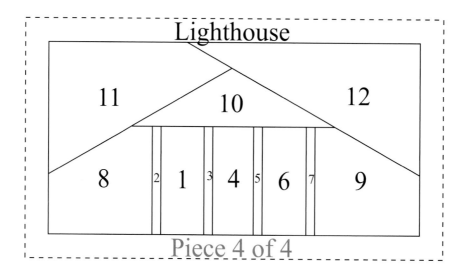

Lighthouse

11   10   12

8 2 1 3 4 5 6 7 9

Piece 4 of 4

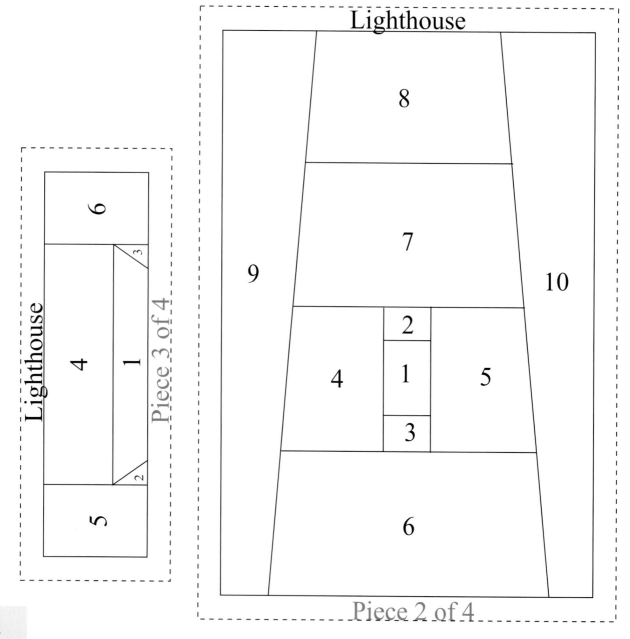

Lighthouse

8

9   7   10

2
4   1   5
3

6

Piece 2 of 4

Lighthouse

6

3
4   1

2
5

Piece 3 of 4

72

Wharf

Finished size 10" x 8"

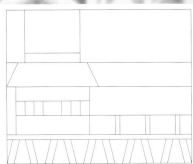

Note: The piecing diagram and pattern pieces are mirror images of the sewn block.

Wharf

10		8						
	1	2	3	4	5	6	7
		9						

Piece 3 of 8

Note: The order for sewing the fabric to the pattern pieces is shown in black. The piecing sequence (1 of 5, 2 of 5, etc.) showing the order to sew the pattern pieces to form the finished block is shown in red.

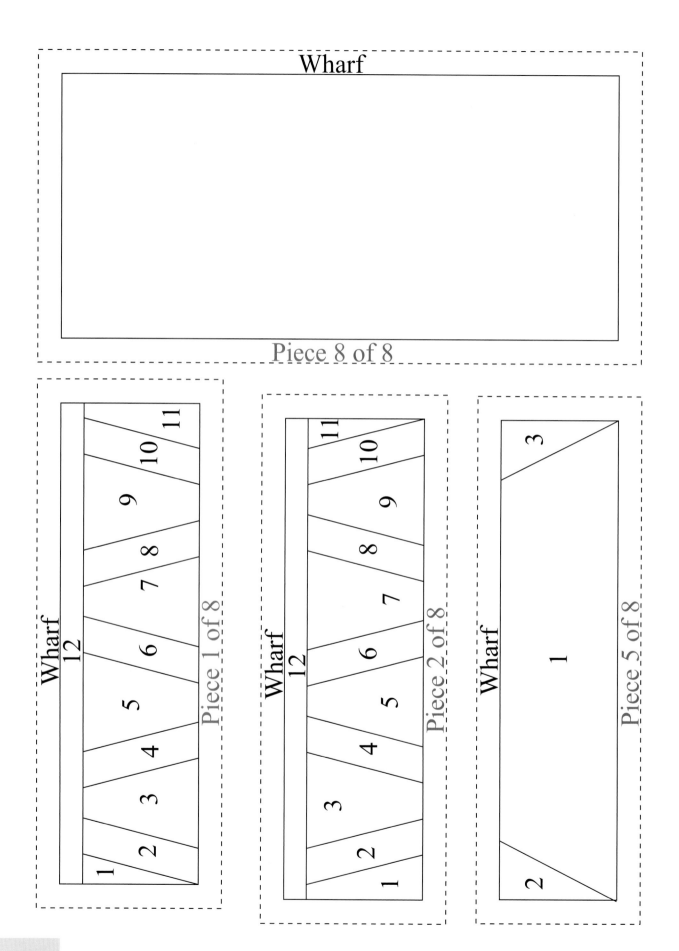

Wharf

Piece 8 of 8

Wharf

Piece 1 of 8

Wharf

Piece 2 of 8

Wharf

Piece 5 of 8

Wharf

Piece 6 of 8

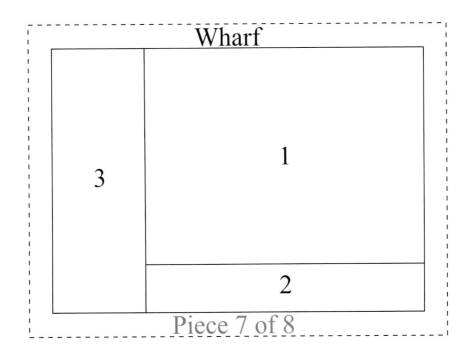

Wharf

3

1

2

Piece 7 of 8

Wharf

8

1

2

3

4

5

6

7

Piece 4 of 8

Skyscraper 1

Finished size 8" x 12"

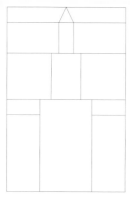

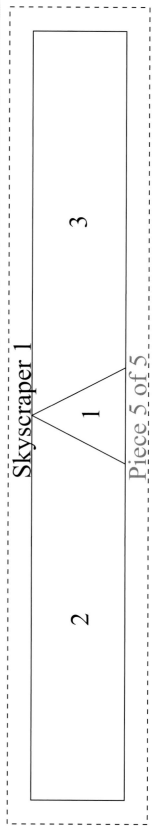

Note: The piecing diagram and pattern pieces are mirror images of the sewn block.

Note: The order for sewing the fabric to the pattern pieces is shown in black. The piecing sequence (1 of 5, 2 of 5, etc.) showing the order to sew the pattern pieces to form the finished block is shown in red.

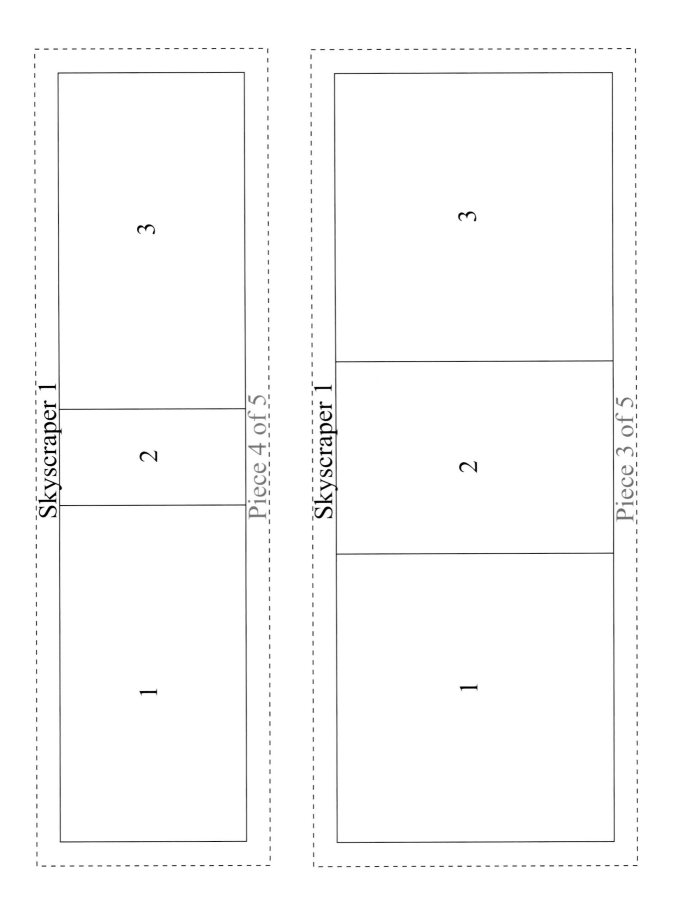

Skyscraper 1

1

2

3

Skyscraper 1

1

2

3

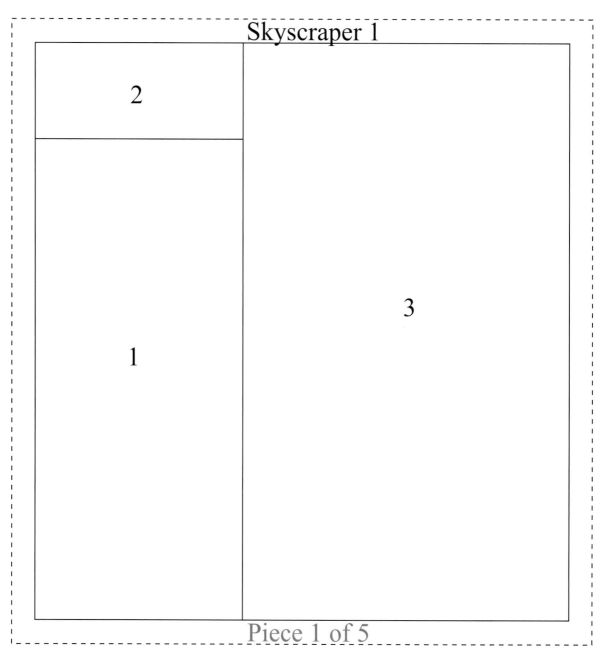

2

1

3

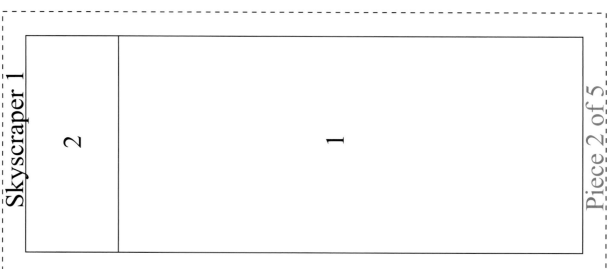

2

1

Skyscraper 2

Finished size 6" x 12"

Note: The piecing diagram and pattern pieces are mirror images of the sewn block.

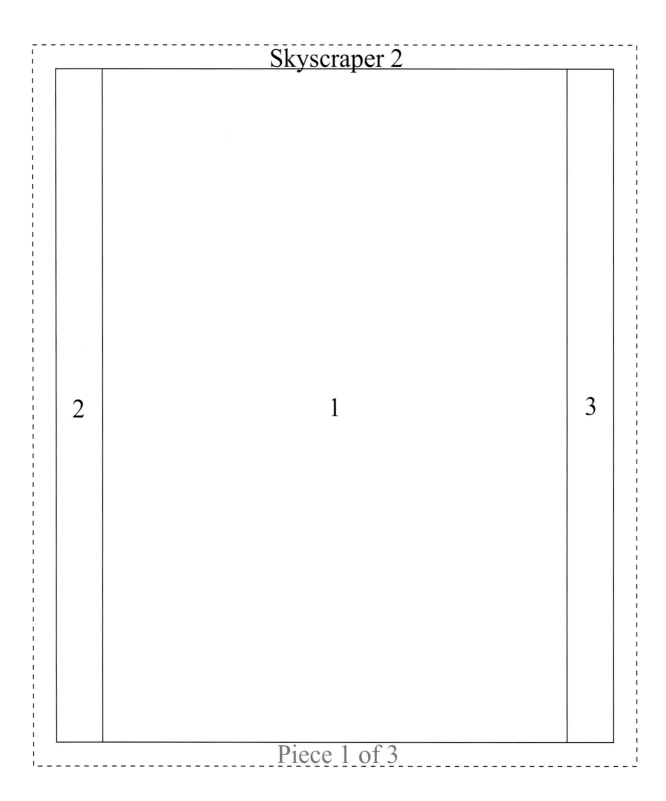

Piece 1 of 3

Note: The order for sewing the fabric to the pattern pieces is shown in black. The piecing sequence (1 of 5, 2 of 5, etc.) showing the order to sew the pattern pieces to form the finished block is shown in red.

Skyscraper 2

4	

2	1	3

Skyscraper 2

2	1	3

4

Skyscraper 3

Finished size 6" x 12"

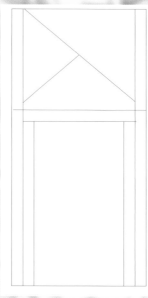

Note: The piecing diagram and pattern pieces are mirror images of the sewn block.

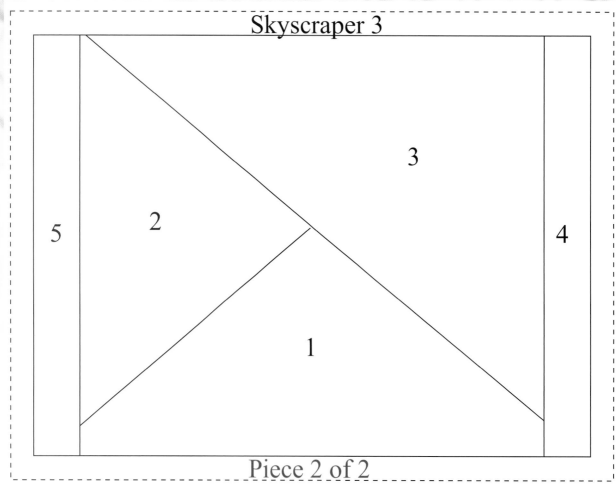

Skyscraper 3

Piece 2 of 2

Skyscraper 3

		4			

5	2	1	3	6

Piece 1 of 2

Note: The order for sewing the fabric to the pattern pieces is shown in black. The piecing sequence (1 of 5, 2 of 5, etc.) showing the order to sew the pattern pieces to form the finished block is shown in red.

Skyscraper 4

Finished size 4" x 12"

Note: The piecing diagram and pattern pieces are mirror images of the sewn block.

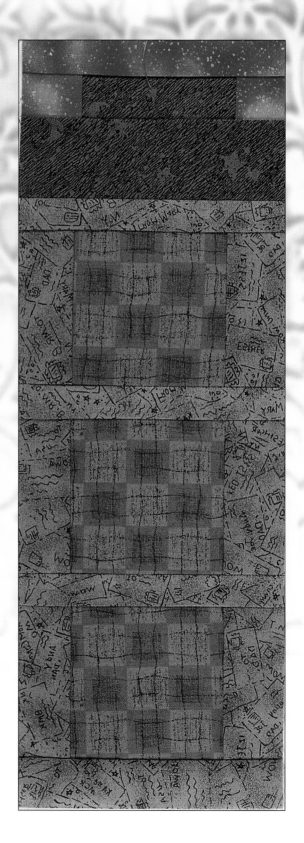

Skyscraper 4

	4	
2	1	3

Piece 2 of 4

Skyscraper 4

	4	
2	1	3
	5	

Piece 1 of 4

Note: The order for sewing the fabric to the pattern pieces is shown in black. The piecing sequence (1 of 5, 2 of 5, etc.) showing the order to sew the pattern pieces to form the finished block is shown in red.

Skyscraper 4

	4	
2	1	3
	5	

Piece 4 of 4

Skyscraper 4

	4	
2	1	3

Piece 3 of 4

Skyscraper 5

Finished size 6" x 12"

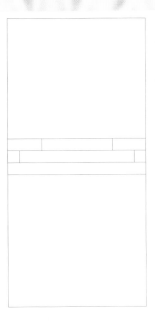

Note: The piecing diagram and pattern pieces are mirror images of the sewn block.

Note: The order for sewing the fabric to the pattern pieces is shown in black. The piecing sequence (1 of 5, 2 of 5, etc.) showing the order to sew the pattern pieces to form the finished block is shown in red.

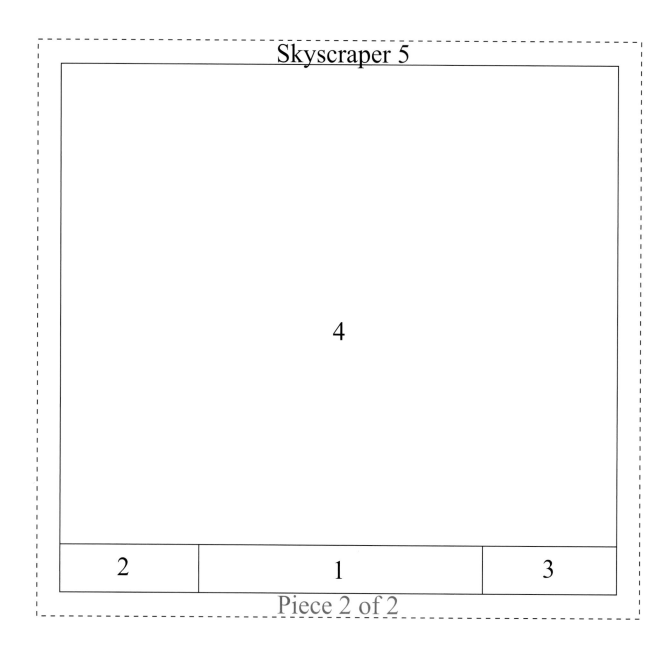

Skyscraper 5

4

| 2 | 1 | 3 |

Piece 2 of 2

Skyscraper 5

| 2 | 1 | 3 |

4

5

Piece 1 of 2

Gazebo

Finished size 4" x 4"

Note: The piecing diagram and pattern pieces are mirror images of the sewn block.

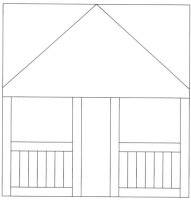

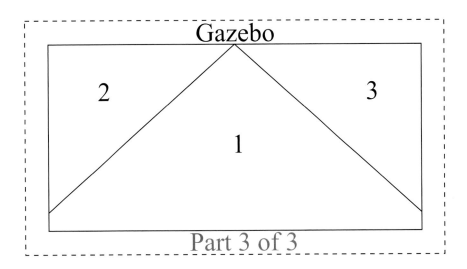

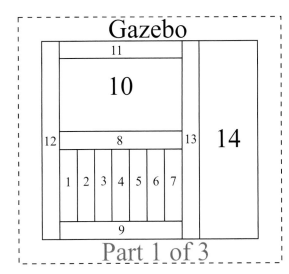

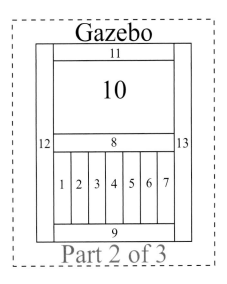

Note: The order for sewing the fabric to the pattern pieces is shown in black. The piecing sequence (1 of 5, 2 of 5, etc.) showing the order to sew the pattern pieces to form the finished block is shown in red.

Hometown Quilts

Barn Yard

Made by Glenda Irvine   Finished size: 36" x 28"

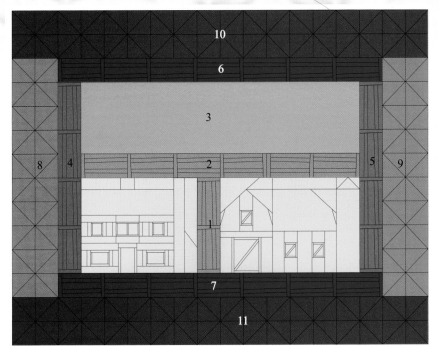

Celebrate farm life—both human and animal—with this quilt. Remember that the finished appliqués will turn out facing opposite the direction of the template.

Materials

3-D Patterns (pages 124-128)
   Cow, Cow Ear • Horse, Horse Ear • Chicken • Pig, Pig Ear
Fabric scraps for the blocks, rail fence and windmill border blocks
6½" x 24½" piece of fabric for section marked Barn Yard Lot in quilt layout diagram
Batting scraps for appliqués
Beads for eyes
Embroidery floss for animal tails
Batting approximately 40" x 32"
Backing approximately 40" x 32"
Binding strips

Instructions

1 Make one each of the following blocks:
   House 1 (page 20)
   Barn (page 55)
Make 24 Rail Fence Border A pieces (page 95)
Make 6 Rail Fence Border B pieces (page 95)
Make 56 Windmill Half Border pieces (this page)

2 Consulting the quilt layout diagram on page 93, stitch together the Rail Fence Border pieces as follows:
   For 1, 2, 3, 6, and 7: 1 piece A and 1 piece B
   For 4 and 8: 1 piece A and 6 piece B
   For 5: 1 piece A and 5 piece B

3 Pair 2 Windmill Half Border pieces and stitch. Press the seam allowance open. Repeat to create 28 Windmill blocks. Stitch a row of 7 Windmill blocks together. Repeat to make 3 sets. Press all seam allowances open.

4 Starting at the left side of section 1 in the quilt layout diagram, stitch a fence section 1 to the left side of the house. Stitch a fence section 2 to the right side of the house. Add the barn, then fence section 3. Press the seam allowances open. Add section 4 to the bottom. Press the seams open.

5 Stitch fence section 5 to one long edge of the barnyard lot piece of fabric. Press the seam allowances open. Add the side fence sections 6 and 7, then the top fence section 8. Press all seam allowances open.

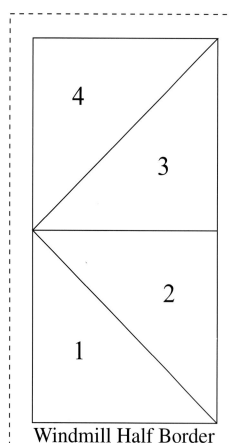

Windmill Half Border

6   Stitch a Windmill Border section to the top and bottom of the quilt top. Press the seam allowances open.

7   Stitch a Windmill Border section to each side of the quilt top. Press the seam allowances open.

8   Remove paper.

9   Following the instructions on page 14, make the animals. Note that the animal will face in the opposite direction from the pattern. Stitch the ears and eyes in place. Tack the animals to the quilt top. For horse tails, tie some short lengths of floss together, trim the raw ends, and take a few stitches to hold in place. For cow tails, group some short lengths (about 5") of floss together and tie a piece of floss around the center. Braid all the pieces together for about 1", then tie off with a piece of floss. Trim the raw ends. Using a few stitches, secure in place. For the pig tail, saturate the floss with glue or a fabric stiffener product. Form into a curl, let dry, and stitch in place.

10   Following the instructions on page 14, use the quick and easy method to complete your quilt.

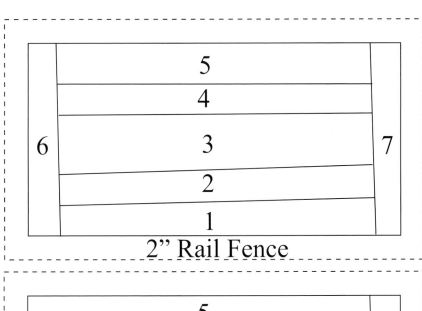

2" Rail Fence

2" Rail Fence

View Through the Window

Finished size: 13" x 15"

Imagine yourself looking out your
window to the house across the street.
Your African violets are blooming on
your windowsill, and your eyelet curtains
are blowing gently in the breeze. That's
the image this little quilt evokes.

Materials

3-D Patterns (pages 124-128)
   Flower Pot • Flower Pot Top • Violet • Violet Leaf
Fabric scraps for the Small Victorian House block, flowers, and flower pots
Sky fabric, cut as follows:
   Pieces 1 and 2 in quilt layout diagram: 2" x 4"
   Piece 3 in quilt layout diagram: 9½" x 3½"
Grass fabric
   Piece 4 in quilt layout diagram: 9½" x 3½"
Four 3" x approximately 35" long strips for window casing (border) pieces
1 yard eyelet border edge fabric
Beads for centers of flowers
Batting approximately 15" x 17"
Backing approximately 15" x 17"

Instructions

1 Make a Small Victorian House block. (page 41)

2 Stitch sky pieces 1 and 2 to the two sides of the house block. Press the seam allowances toward the sky pieces.

3 Stitch the sky piece 3 to the top of the house/side sky pieces. Press the seam allowances toward the top sky piece.

4 Stitch the grass piece 4 to the bottom of the house/sky. Press the seam allowances toward the grass piece.

5 Remove the paper from the house block.

6 For the curtains, cut two pieces of eyelet fabric 7" x 10", having the shorter measurement along the fancy finished border edge of the fabric. Press under 1/8" along one long edge of each curtain and topstitch one on the left side and one on the right. These will be the inside edges of the curtains.

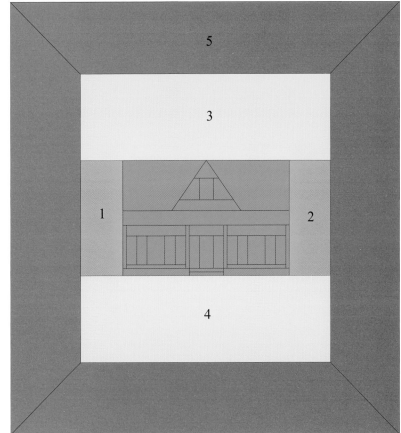

7 For the window valance, cut a piece of the eyelet fabric 4" x 16", having the 16" measurement along the border (fancy finished edge) of the eyelet fabric. Along the opposite long edge, run a double row of long gathering stitches just each side of 1/4" from the raw edge.

8 Lay the two curtain pieces on the quilt top, matching the side and top edges exactly as they will appear on the finished quilt. Baste.

9 Lay the valance on top, matching the top long edge, pulling up the stitches to make the gathers fit the allotted space, and matching the side edges to the side of the quilt. Baste.

10 Following the instructions on page 13, add the mitered border to the quilt, including the curtain edges in the seams along the edge of the quilt.

11 Follow the instructions on page 14 to make the three-dimensional flowerpots and flowers for your quilt. Sew the beads to the centers of the flowers. Tack to the quilt.

12 Turn to page 15 for instructions for sandwiching, quilting, and binding your quilt.

Row Houses

Finished size: 25" x 17"

What could be a snapshot from any number of city neighborhoods, this quilt conjures up the sounds of life growing up on an urban street.

Materials

Fabric scraps for the house blocks

Two 1" x 8" strips for inner border sides, numbers 1 and 2 on quilt layout diagram (black print in photo)

Two 1" x 17" strips for inner border top and bottom, numbers 3 and 4 in quilt layout diagram

Two 4½" x 9½" border pieces for sides, numbers 5 and 6 in quilt layout diagram

Two 4½" x 25½" border pieces for top and bottom, numbers 7 and 8 on quilt layout diagram

Batting approximately 25" x 19"

Backing approximately 25" x 19"

Binding strips

Instructions

1 Make the 4 row house blocks (pages 58, 60, 62, 64).

2 Stitch the row houses together side-by-side as shown in the quilt layout diagram. Press the seams open.

3 Stitch the 2 inner border side strips, numbered 1 and 2, to the 2 side edges of the houses. Press the seams open.

4 Stitch the 2 inner border top and bottom strips, numbered 3 and 4, to the top and bottom of the houses unit. Press seam allowances open.

5 Stitch the 2 border side strips, numbered 5 and 6, to the 2 side edges of the house section. Press the seams open.

6 Stitch the 2 border side strips, numbered 7 and 8, to the top and bottom edges of the house section. Press the seams open.

7 Remove the paper from the row house blocks.

8 Prepare the quilt sandwich, quilt, and bind as instructed on page 15.

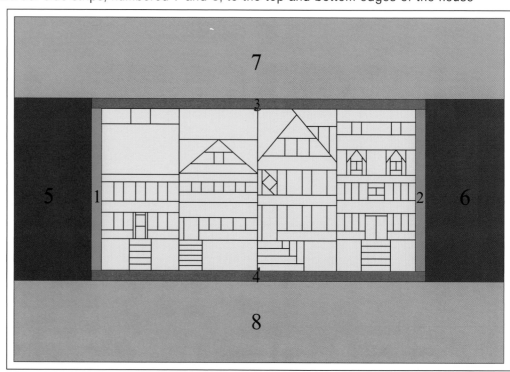

Ocean Waves

Made by Glenda Irvine   Finished size: 24" x 28"

*Dig into your blue scraps and stash
to make this slice of seaside life.*

Materials

Fabric scraps for the blocks and ocean waves sections
Batting approximately 28" x 32"
Backing approximately 28" x 32"
Binding strips

Instructions

1   Make one each of the following blocks:
    Cape Cod House (page 46)
    Wharf (page 73)
    Light House (page 71)
Make 48 Double Ocean Waves pieces (page 103)
Make 20 Single Ocean Waves pieces (page 103)

2   Consulting the quilt layout diagram, piece together the double and single ocean waves pieces to form the ocean waves sections.

3   Again consulting the quilt layout diagram, piece the blocks and ocean waves sections together in the numbered sequence.

4   First sew the Cape Cod house and adjoining Ocean Waves section together. Press seam allowance open. This creates section 1. Now sew Ocean Waves section 2 to section 1. Press the seam allowances open. Stitch the Wharf block and the Ocean Waves section together to form section 3. Press the seam open. Stitch section 3 to section 2. Press the seam open. Continue on to section 4. Sew on the border sections.

5   Remove the paper.

6   Following the instructions on page 14, use the quick and easy method to complete your quilt.

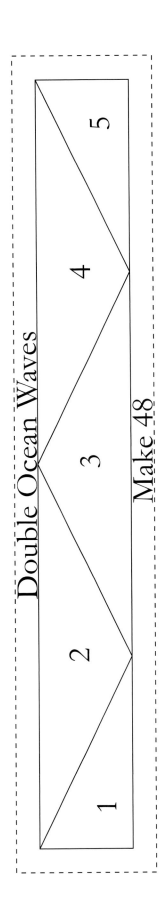

Double Ocean Waves

1 2 3 4 5

Make 48

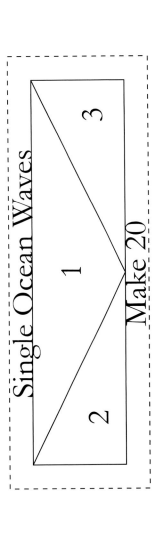

Single Ocean Waves

2 1 3

Make 20

Spring

Finished size: 24¾" x 15¾"

Tulips bloom and birds sit on their eggs in this spring scene. You may substitute any house you wish for your quilt.

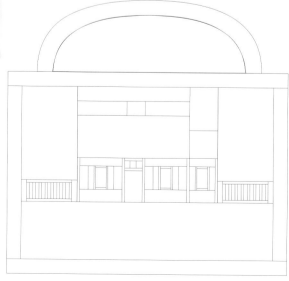

Materials

3-D Patterns (pages 124-128)
   Crescent Sky, Crescent Border
   Sun, Sun Smile
   Tulip, Tulip Leaf
   Bird Nest
   Bird, Bird Wing

Scraps for house, picket fence blocks and appliqués
Two pieces of sky fabric 4½" x 6½", numbered 2 and 4 in quilt layout diagram
One foreground piece 16½" x 4½" numbered 5
Two border pieces 1½" x 12½" numbered 6 and 7 in quilt layout diagram
Two border pieces 1½" x 19½", numbered 8 and 9 in quilt layout diagram
One sky piece using Crescent Sky template
One border piece using Crescent Border template
Batting approximately 29" x 20"
Backing approximately 29" x 20"
Scraps of batting for appliqués
Shank buttons for the sun's eyes

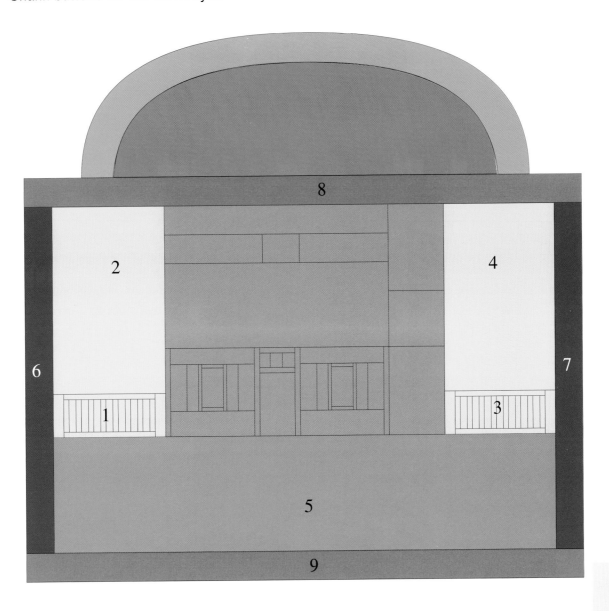

Instructions

1 Make one House 4 block (page 29) and two Picket Fence blocks (page 67).

2 For each of the Picket Fence blocks, stitch the short edge of a Sky piece, numbered 2 and 4 in the quilt layout diagram, to one long edge of a Picket Fence piece. Press the seam allowances toward the Sky.

3 Stitch a Picket Fence/Sky section to each side of the house block. Press the seam allowances open.

4 Stitch the foreground piece, numbered 5 in the quilt layout diagram, to the bottom of the House/Picket Fences. Press the seam allowances toward the foreground.

5 Stitch the two border side pieces, numbered 6 and 7, to the two side edges of the House/Picket Fence/foreground. Press the seams toward the border.

6 Stitch the two border top and bottom strips, numbered 8 and 9, to the top and bottom of the House/Picket Fence/foreground unit. Press seam allowances toward the border.

7 Stitch the Crescent Sky piece to the Crescent Border piece. Press the seam allowances toward the border.

8 Center at the top of the quilt and stitch, starting and ending 1/4" from the ends. Press the seam open.

9 Remove the paper from the house picket fence blocks.

10 Make the appliqués as instructed on page 14. Sew the eyes and mouth to the sun. Tack the appliqués to the quilt top.

11 Finish your quilt using the easy wallhanging method on page 14.

Summer

Finished size: 23" square

A wreath of flowers surrounds our house
in this summery quilt. After you make
your border blocks, lay them wrong
(printed) side up in their proper
assemblage and it'll be easy to see how to
piece them together.

Materials

3-D Patterns (pages 124-128)
   Flower #1, Flower #2, Flower Center, Flower Petals, Leaf
Fabric scraps to make the house block
Background fabric:
Two pieces 6" x 10½", numbered 1 and 2 in quilt layout diagram
Two pieces 4" x 17¼", numbered 3 and 4 in quilt layout diagram
Scraps of background fabric for border
Two 1" x 17¼" strips for side inner border
Two 1" x 18¼" strips for top and bottom inner border
Fat quarters of the binding/inner border fabric for the outer (paper pieced) border
Fat quarter of second fabric for outer border
Assorted fabric scraps for appliqué flowers and leaves
Buttons or beads for flower centers
Batting approximately 27" x 27"
Backing approximately 27" x 27"

Instructions

1 Make one Cape Cod House block (page 46).

2 Stitch background pieces 1 and 2 to the top and bottom of the house block. Press the seam allowances toward the background pieces.

3 Stitch background pieces 3 and 4 to the sides. Press the seam allowances open.

4 Stitch the side inner border strips to the sides of the quilt top. Press seams toward background.

5 Stitch the top and bottom inner border strips to the top and bottom of the quilt top. Press seams toward background.

6 Make 24 Summer Border pieces and two Summer Border Corner pieces. Piece them together following the quilt layout diagram.

7 Sew the pieced Border to the quilt top, stopping and starting the stitching 1/4" from the raw edge.

8 Following the instructions on page 14, make the Flower and Leaf appliqués and sew them to the quilt.

9 Following the instructions on page 16, sandwich, quilt and bind your quilt.

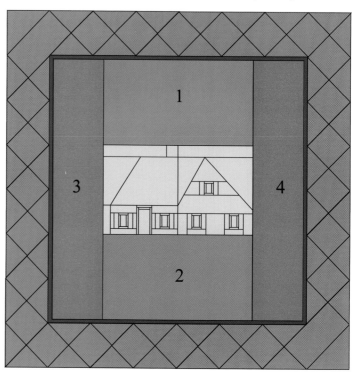

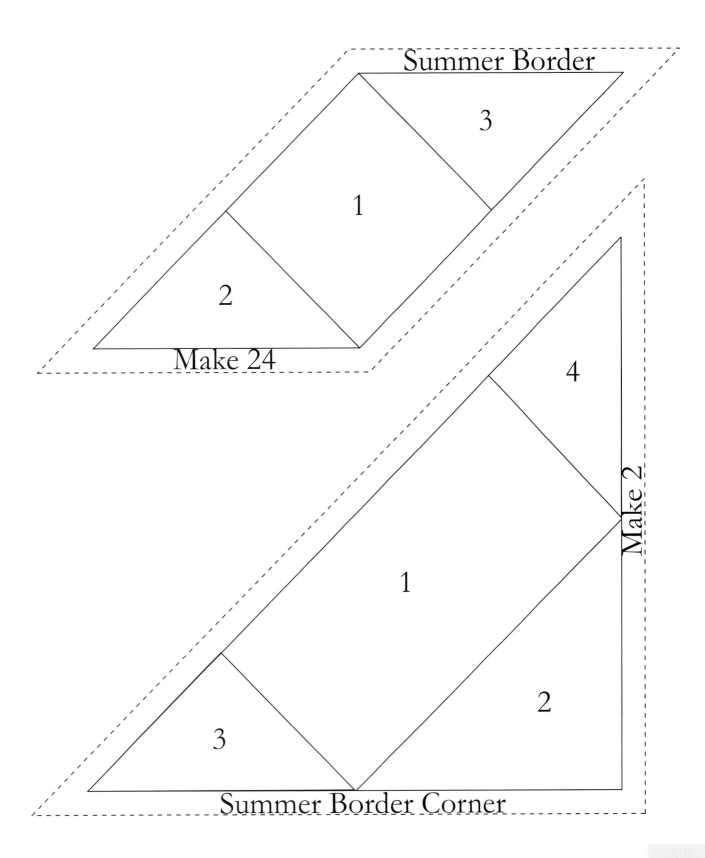

Summer Border

3

1

2

Make 24

4

Make 2

1

2

3

Summer Border Corner

Autumn

Finished Size: 22½" x 15"

It's a not-so-scary Halloween on this autumn quilt. A friendly ghost hangs in the tree with a bright moon lighting up the fun.

Materials

3-D Patterns (ages 124-128)
   Tree Trunk, Tree Top
   Pumpkin #1, Pumpkin #2
   Apple Basket
   Moon
Fabric scraps to make house block and appliqués
Red shank buttons for apples
White fabric, quarter-size piece of batting, and bit of embroidery floss for ghost
Two 4½" x 8½" pieces of background fabric, numbered 1 and 2 in quilt layout diagram
Two 1¼" x 8½" inner border strips, numbered 3 and 4 in quilt layout diagram
Two 1¼" x 18" inner border strips, numbered 5 and 6 in quilt layout diagram
Two 3½" x 10" outer border pieces, numbered 7 and 8
Two 3½" x 24" outer border pieces, numbered 9 and 10
Batting approximately 26" x 19"
Backing approximately 26" x 19"

Instructions

1   Make one Large Victorian House block (page 43).

2   Stitch the two background pieces, numbered 1 and 2, to the sides of the house block. Press the seams toward the background fabric.

3   Stitch the two inner border strips, numbered 3 and 4, to the sides of these background pieces. Press the seam allowances toward the background pieces.

Instructions continued on page 112

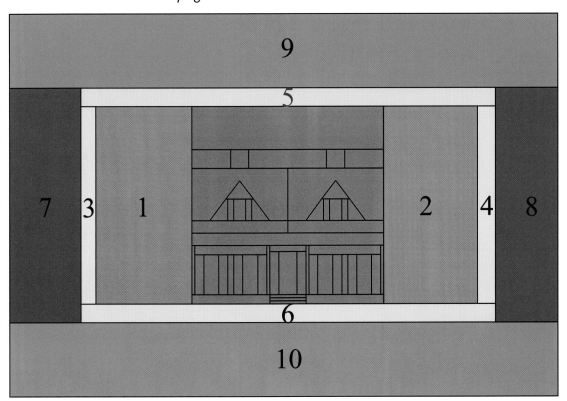

4 Stitch the two remaining inner border pieces, numbered 5 and 6, to the top and bottom. Press seam allowances toward the background pieces.

5 Stitch the outer border pieces, numbered 7 and 8, to the sides of the quilt top. Press the seam allowances toward the border.

6 Stitch the outer border pieces, numbered 9 and 10, to the top and bottom of the quilt top. Press the seam allowances toward the border.

7 Following the instructions on page 14, make the appliqués and tack them to the quilt top.

8 Following the instructions starting on page 14, use the quick and easy method to finish your quilt.

9 To make the ghost, use pinking shears to cut a 5" circle of the white fabric. Using the embroidery floss, baste a 1½" wide circle on the center. Pull up on the gather stitches and insert the batting. Tighten and knot the floss. Tack to the tree on the quilt.

10 Sew the apple buttons in the basket.

Winter

Finished Size: 24" x 28"

Snow falling, a star shining, a picture perfect winter night scene.

Materials

3-D Patterns (pages 124-128)
Star, Tree Top, Tree Tier
Fabric scraps to make the Church Block, and the Star and Tree appliqués
Sky fabric:
Two pieces 4½" x 10½"
One piece 18½" x 12½"
Border fabric:
Four pieces 3½" x approximately 36" long
5mm white pompoms
1/2" white pompoms
One bell
Batting approximately 28" x 32"
Backing approximately 28" x 32"

Instructions

1 Make one Church block (page 49).

2 Stitch the Sky pieces, numbered 1 and 2 on the quilt layout diagram, to the sides of the Church block. Press the seam allowances toward the sky.

3 Stitch the large Sky piece, number 3 in the quilt layout diagram to the top edge of the Church block/side sky pieces. Press the seam allowances toward the Sky piece.

4 Remove the paper from the Sky block.

5 Following the instructions on page 13, apply the mitered border.

6 Following the instructions on page 14, make the Star and Tree appliqués. Tack them in place.

7 Tack the pompom snowflakes and the bell to the quilt top.

8 Turn to page 14 for the quick and easy wallhanging method of making your top into a quilt. Quilt as desired.

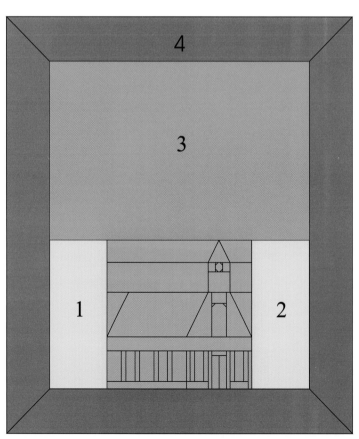

Log Cabins

Finished size: 34" x 44"

The rich jewel-like colors of the Hoffman Batik fabrics I used for this quilt give it a very special, rich look. I used three or four fabrics of a color for the log cabins, plus the contrasts (window and door trim, windows, door) and the roof. The background is just one delicious gold hand dye. Several of the suppliers listed in the Sources section sell fat quarter selections of batiks, and one sells six-inch squares. I used one fabric for the chimneys, inner border, and the binding.

Materials

For the blocks:

Three or four fabrics each: yellow, blue, green, orange, pink, and purple

Fabric scraps for roofs, windows, doors and trims

From background fabric:

Three 2½" x 8½" strips, numbered 1, 2, and 3

Four 2½" x 18½" strips, numbered 4, 5, 6, and 7

Two 2½" x 32½" strips, numbered 8 and 9

Two 5½" x 34½" strips, numbered 14 and 15

Two 5½" x 34½" strips, numbered 16 and 17

From the inner border fabric (brown in photographed quilt)

Two 1½" x 32½" strips, numbered 10 and 11

Two 1½" x 24½" strips, numbered 12 and 13

Binding strips

Batting approximately 38" x 48"

Backing approximately 38" x 48"

Instructions

1 Make six Log Cabin blocks (page 68).

2 Lay out the blocks as you wish them to be for the finished quilt top. Stitch a strip (number 1, 2, or 3 in the quilt layout diagram) between each set. Press the seam allowances toward the strips.

3 Follow the quilt layout diagram to stitch pieces numbered 4, 5, 6, and 7 to the tops and bottoms of the blocks as shown in the diagram to join all of the blocks together. Press the seam allowances toward the strips.

4 Stitch the strip pieces numbered 8 and 9 to the sides. Press the seam allowances toward the strips.

5 Stitch the inner border (brown in photo of quilt) strips, numbered 10 and 11, to the sides. Press the seam allowances toward the strips.

6 Stitch the inner border strips, numbered 12 and 13, to the top and bottom. Press the seam allowances toward the strips.

7 Stitch the outer border (gold in the photo) strips, numbered 14 and 15, to the sides. Press the seam allowances toward the strips.

8 Stitch the outer border strips numbered 16 and 17 to the top and bottom. Press the seam allowances toward the strips.

9 Remove the paper.

10 As instructed on page 16, make your quilt sandwich, quilt and bind the quilt.

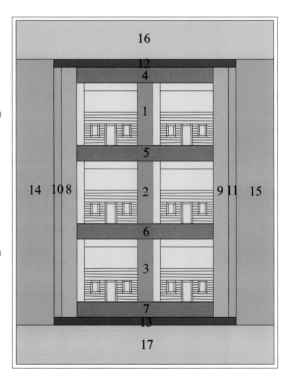

Gallery of Quilts

Pacific Rim Redux

By Susanne McCoy

Pretty Maids All In a Row

By Nancy Phelps Goins

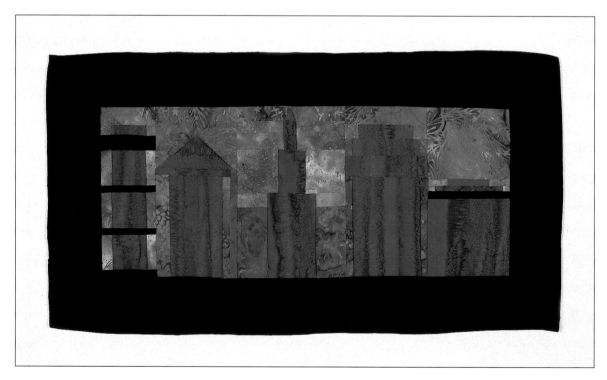

Sunset Over The City

By Grace Grimsley

By the Sea

By June Dale

New York Skyline

By Marcia Kessler

"As seen from my hometown - Governor's Island"

Untitled

By Margo Antonoff

"It's a Jungle Out There"

By Annie Weinstein

Sources

Mail Order Shopping

Nothing beats visiting a quilt shop to see all the latest sewn samples and fondle the enticing new fabrics. Believe me, I help the local shops thrive. But there's never enough fabric and quilting goodies for my appetite, so... I spread my quilting dollars far and wide both online and through mail order shopping, thereby visiting quilt stores I may never see in real life.

These are the suppliers and online resources I use and have found to be dependable. In fact to test this for you, I ordered fabric from two of them one morning and received my orders in the same mail delivery the following week!

Keepsake Quilting
Route 25B
PO Box 1618
Centre Harbor, NH 03226-1618
(800) 865-9458
Call for a free catalog.

This hefty little catalog is chock-full of all the latest and tried and true quilt notions, gadgets, patterns, books, fabric and handy fabric medleys too. No wonder it is entitled, "The Quilter's Wishbook!"

Connecting Threads
PO Box 8940
Vancouver, WA 98668-8940
(800) 574-6454
Call for a free catalog.

Books and patterns take center stage in this catalog. Rulers, rotary cutters and every other quilting supply round out the selection, all at discounted prices.

Hancock's of Paducah
3841 Hinkleville Rd.
Paducah, KY 42001
(800) 845-8723
http:www.Hancocks-Paducah.com
Order a catalog online or via the toll-free number.

A delicious selection of the latest fabrics from the best manufacturers and designers, plus threads, quilting gadgets, batting and more, all at great prices. Check out both the online and paper catalogs since one may have fabrics the other doesn't.

Quilts and Other Comforts
1 Quilters Lane
PO Box 4100
Golden, CO 80401-0100
(800) 881-6624
Call for a free catalog.

"The catalog for quilt lovers" focuses on fabrics and patterns, with a good selection of the most popular books and all those wonderful quilt tools as well. You'll find some nice quilty gift-type items.

Online Resources

You'll find fabrics, books, tools and notions at the following online sources. I've ordered from them all, online, with great success. You may use the secure server. (It's very easy, just follow the online instructions.) Online orders are acknowledged with e-mails telling you your order was received, what was ordered, and the total amount. Pretty neat! If you think online ordering is impersonal, have no fear, each of these businesses is run by quilters, just like us, who love quilts. I have corresponded with each of them and heard only excellent reviews from other online quilters. Or, if you're not convinced this is safe (I am!) call with your order and credit card information.

When fabric shopping, I print out the online fabric swatches. Then I have a visual record not only of what I ordered, but I staple these print-outs to my quilt design so I know exactly how I intended to use them in the quilt.

Bighorn Quilts
608 Greybull Ave.
PO Box 566
Greybull, WY 82426
(877) 586-9150
http://www.bighornquilts.com

At this online fabric store, fabric certainly does take center stage. And lots of it, all at, "Well, I can't resist," prices.

Pine Tree Quiltworks, Ltd.
585 Broadway
South Portland, ME 04107
(207) 799-7357
http://www.pinetree.quiltworks.com
Or call for a free catalog.

A complete quilt shop including a wonderful selection of fabrics and every notion imaginable, all at discounted prices. There is also a traditional mail order catalog available.

Quilt-a-way Fabrics
540 Back Westminster Road
Westminster, VT 05150
(802) 722-4743
http://www.quiltaway.com

A full service quilt shop, Quilt-a-way's mail order site offers a great selection of fabrics at the lowest possible prices, including many batiks.

Online Resources

Following are a few starting points for exploring quilting and foundation piecing in the wonderful world of cyberspace.

PC Piecers
http://www.bankswith.appollotrust.com/larryb/PCPiecers.htm

Dedicated specifically to foundation piecing, the PC Piecers' site has a lot of great information, patterns, and activities—and links to many other foundation piecing sites and goodies.

Zippy Designs Publishing
Home of The Foundation Piecer Magazine
RR 1 Box 187M
Newport, VA 24128
(540) 544-7153
http://www.zippydesigns.com

There is a magazine devoted exclusively to foundation piecing—the creation of husband and wife team Elizabeth Schwartz and Stephen Seifert, The Foundation Piecer is a lovely, full color bimonthly, full of inspired patterns (all included and to size.) And don't miss the Zippy Designs' web site. You will find a schoolhouse of foundation piecing instructions, block patterns, information about their magazine, products and much more.

Judy Smith's Quilting, Needlearts and Antiques Page
http://www.quiltart.com/judy

Judy is an online quilter from way back, and has a highly acclaimed site of great quilting links. Starting your search with Judy's site, you'll quickly accrue a long list of bookmarked favorites!

About.com
http://quilting.about.com

The mission of About.com is to be the place to go to learn about any topic. Each site is devoted to a specific area of interest and is hosted by a real, live, accessible human being. And Susan Druding's Quilting site does just that. It's a resource for all facets of quilting, offering how-to's, FAQ's, sources, links to other sites and much, much more.

Missing Fabrics Page
http://www.missingfabrics.com

The missing fabrics page works, proving once again how kind and caring quilters are. I ran out of fabric for a quilt that started as a wallhanging and decided it had to be bed-size. Since it had been produced two seasons before, no local or online shops had any of the fabrics I needed. So, I scanned it and posted it on the missing fabrics page. Lo and behold a quilter in Canada spotted it on the site and sent her friend, who lived closer to town, to fetch me some from their local quilt shop.

...And don't forget to visit me at my cyberhome: www.iejodie.com

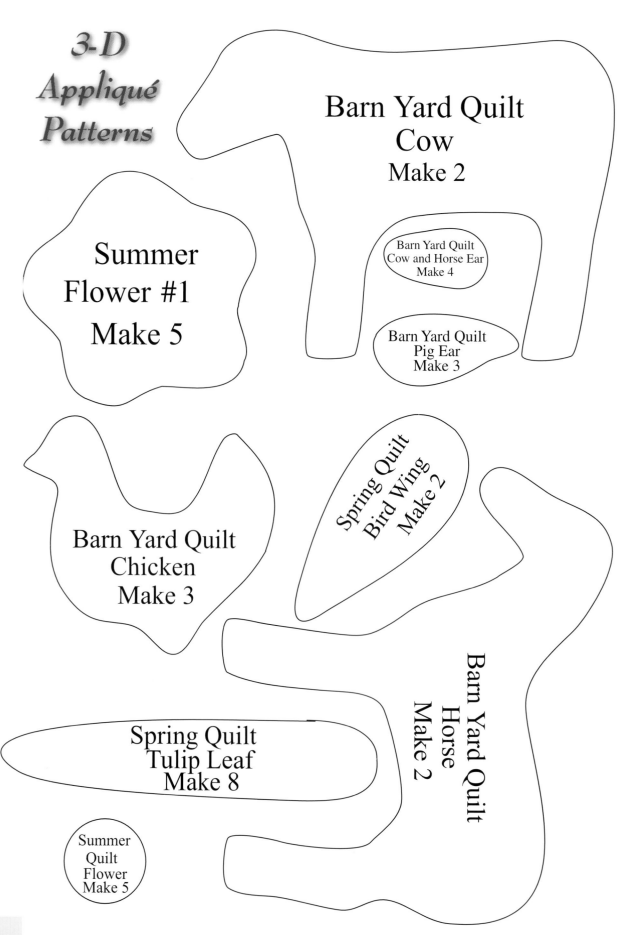

3-D Appliqué Patterns

Barn Yard Quilt
Cow
Make 2

Summer
Flower #1
Make 5

Barn Yard Quilt
Cow and Horse Ear
Make 4

Barn Yard Quilt
Pig Ear
Make 3

Barn Yard Quilt
Chicken
Make 3

Spring Quilt
Bird Wing
Make 2

Barn Yard Quilt
Horse
Make 2

Spring Quilt
Tulip Leaf
Make 8

Summer
Quilt
Flower
Make 5

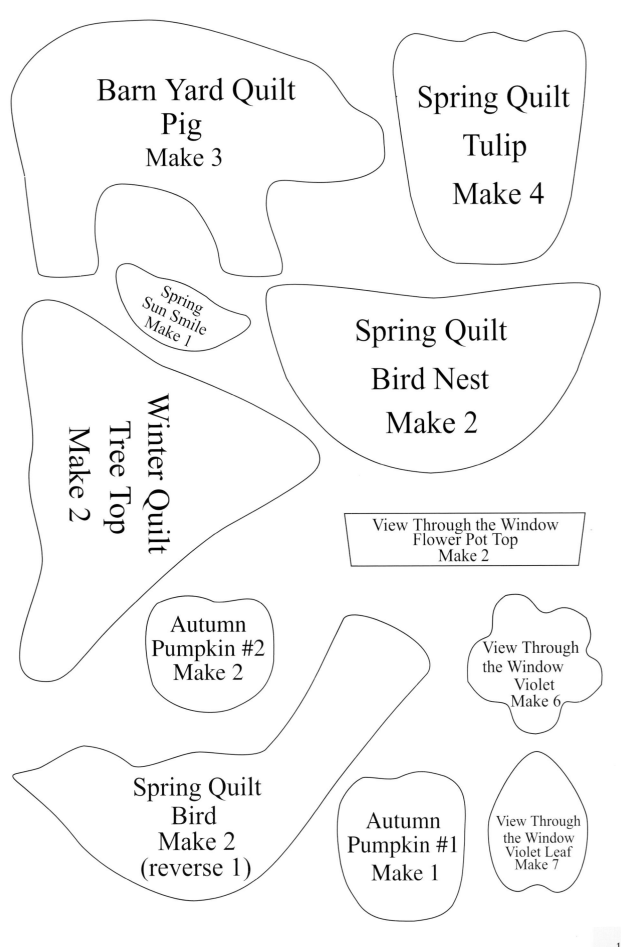

Barn Yard Quilt
Pig
Make 3

Spring Quilt
Tulip
Make 4

Spring
Sun Smile
Make 1

Spring Quilt
Bird Nest
Make 2

Winter Quilt
Tree Top
Make 2

View Through the Window
Flower Pot Top
Make 2

Autumn
Pumpkin #2
Make 2

View Through
the Window
Violet
Make 6

Spring Quilt
Bird
Make 2
(reverse 1)

Autumn
Pumpkin #1
Make 1

View Through
the Window
Violet Leaf
Make 7

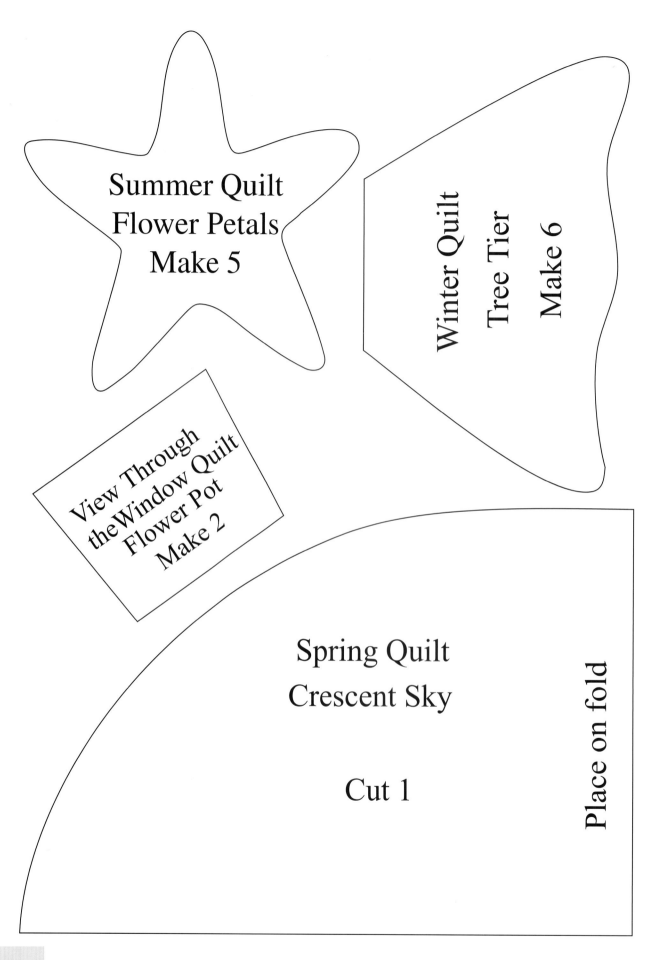

Summer Quilt
Flower Petals
Make 5

Winter Quilt
Tree Tier
Make 6

View Through
theWindow Quilt
Flower Pot
Make 2

Spring Quilt

Crescent Sky

Cut 1

Place on fold